بسم الله الرحمن الرحيم

This book is not subject to copyright.

Abdussabur Kirke asserts the moral right to be identified as its author.

Lifeboat Press

Contact: abdussabur.kirke@gmail.com

ISBN: 978-0-7961-4950-3
Manufactured in the United Kingdom

ENTER ISLAM

An Invitation

Abdussabur Kirke

LIFEBOAT PRESS

CONTENTS

Islam 7
Muhammad, the Messenger of Allah............ 21
Five Pillars... 37
Idols 61
Transmission 81
Transformation 89
The Path 97
Riba 119
Christianity.. 141
Qur'an... 151
Marriage 157
War 163
The Judgment... 169
Islam is with the Muslims, not in books..... 175

ISLAM

This book is written for you. It is directed at you. It is about the call of Islam to you. If you intend to look at Islam purely for information purposes, this is the wrong book.

The call of Islam is a call from Reality, to come to Reality. It is not the subject of detached study from outside. It is something to engage with. To study it is to take steps towards it. To understand it is to enter it. To study it and go away from it is to fail to understand it – or to be unwilling to accept it.

Absolute Reality IS Allah. If you say about Allah, "That is not real," then it is not Allah you are negating. Allah is your Origin and your Destination. Allah is Absolute Singularity. The world is multifarious. Allah is One. It is passing. Allah is permanent. It is conditional. Allah is not subject to conditions.

Knowing Allah is therefore the mirror act of knowing the world. And to know the world for what it really is – not for what it purports to be – is to know Allah, because the world is Allah's opposite. Inasmuch as I become cognisant of my mortality, I become cognisant of Allah's Permanence. While I am still lost in the illusion of my permanence, I am veiled from knowing Allah.

The journey you must therefore take – if you intend to take it – is the abandonment of your insistence on the world. That is what Islam is for. But as we shall see, Islam requires engagement with the world. You have to give the world its due.

Once you engage with Islam properly – or you could say once you accept its engagement with you – then the journey can begin.

But Islam is not the aim. It is the means. Reality is the aim. Allah says in His Book, the Noble Qur'an:

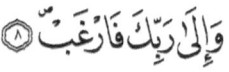

Make your Lord your goal.

This is not something to get your head around,

because your head can never get around it. You have to put your head on the floor. The word Islam means submission. It also means peace, but not in the pacifist sense or being nice, compliant citizens. No. Submission is to admit that you don't know.

Furthermore, Islam is to recognise that there is someone who does know: the Messenger of Allah, Muhammad, may Allah bless him and grant him peace. He is the one who knows. He is the door to knowledge, because his submission to Allah was perfect. He reaches and embodies the limits of human possibility. He did not attain this station by his own achievement, although whatever good human characteristics can be achieved by one's own efforts, he achieved them. He was created in the form of 'al-Amin' – the Trustworthy – which was the name by which he was known among his people before he received Revelation. They knew he could be trusted in an absolute way – or, you could say, he could not be mistrusted without betraying oneself. So when Revelation came, only those insistent on their own superiority or entrenched in their own positions could deny it.

And that remains the case today.

His blessed wife Aisha, may Allah be pleased with her, said, "His character was the Qur'an." The word for character in the Arabic is khuluq, which is from the same root as 'to create'. He was created as the human actuation of Allah's words.

My Master, may Allah have mercy on him, used to say about this, "The Messenger of Allah, Muhammad, may Allah bless him and grant him peace, was the Qur'an walking."

At one end of the spectrum of human experience is to see yourself as willing and deciding, the shaper of your destiny. At the other is realising your utter subjugation to the Decree. Each of these modes has its time and place. The former is the description befitting the world: "I decide. The things that happen to me are result of my decisions and the decisions of others." The latter is the description befitting Reality: "Allah decides. Allah has given me everything."

When I met my Master, may Allah reward him, he welcomed me at the door. His words were warm and he touched with humour on light subjects. Only later, once we were sitting down and had passed through the doorway of courtesy, did he bring up more serious things. Allah had put him in the footsteps of Muhammad, may Allah bless him and grant him peace, and Islam is nothing other than following Muhammad in what he did, his courtesies, his likes and dislikes, what he ordered, what he allowed and what he disallowed. Putting oneself under obedience to Muhammad, may Allah bless him and grant him peace, is synonymous with putting oneself under obedience to Allah.

This is not to equate Muhammad, may Allah bless him and grant him peace, with Allah. On the contrary. Allah cannot be equated or mingled or associated with anything. Muhammad, may Allah bless him and grant him peace, is – as every practising Muslim says in their prayers many times a day – the slave of Allah. He insisted on this description.

We too, whether Muslim or not, are slaves of Allah. Everyone's slavehood to Allah is total. Allah decrees – we are decreed. But from another point of view, slavehood is on a scale from complete, which was the station of the Messenger of Allah and all of the Prophets and Messengers, to absolute rejection of slavehood, which is the station of the kafir, the one who rejects Reality. The kafir is still a slave, but he not only doesn't know it, he actively positions himself against it and expends himself in designating himself master over himself.

Kufr, the attribute of the kafir, is not a religious category made up by priests or some other people of the past. It is one of the innate human possibilities. Islam means submission. Kufr comes from the

Arabic word meaning to reject, but also to cover over. It is a condition people are in when they will not accept Reality. The kafir covers over the way things are.

Acceptance from Allah is through the door of obedience to the Messenger, may Allah bless him and grant him peace. This is part of the human design. Obedience to the Messenger is by following what one comes to know of him and his actions, and loving him.

Islam is based on five Pillars.

The first pillar of Islam, the Shahada, is to say, in the presence of at least two witnesses:

أَشْهَدُ أَن لَّا إِلَهَ إِلَّا اللهُ
وَأَشْهَدُ أَنَّ مُحَمَّدًا رَسُولُ اللهِ

Ash-hadu an la ilaha illallah
Wa ash-hadu anna Muhammadan Rasulullah

I testify that there is no god except Allah
And I testify that Muhammad
is the Messenger of Allah.

This Arabic is the pure language spoken by the Messenger of Allah, and those are the exact words he taught to his Companions.

ASH-HADU AN LA ILAHA ILLALLAH

I testify that there is no 'ilah' – except Allah. 'Ilah' is that which everything needs but which has no need of anything. It is more than what the word 'god' normally signifies.

No god. Only Allah.

In other words, saying the Shahada is, "I say to you people gathered that I turn my back not only on other gods, but on any other thing to which one might ascribe divinity or incline towards with the inclination of worship: absolute power, absolute life, absolute knowledge, absolute hearing, absolute seeing, absolute speaking, the absolute ability to decree how things are – either good or bad. Moreover, I turn my back on any idea of anything other than Allah having any absolute permanence or reality. I turn my back on all that – and I affirm the One Who owns all of that."

"Most of all, I turn my back, therefore, on myself. I do not know. These people, the Muslims – the Submitters – know something I do not, but I want to know. I do not ultimately decree my own journey, my own experience or my own outcome. If I look carefully and clearly, after stilling the noise and turbulence of my self, I admit that I don't really determine my own choices. It is Allah who does so, through the means of the things I experience as choice, events and history. The thing I experience as choice takes place at the meeting between the particular self-form with which I arrive at a given moment and the circumstances of that moment, which are due to Allah through the means of the extraordinary effulgence of creation and the events in it, over which Allah is the Master in every moment. I have seen this, and I testify to it. I have taken the step."

That is what it means to say the first line of the Shahada.

Muhyiddin Ibn 'Arabi, whom the Muslims have called the Greatest Shaykh, said that Allah governs creation from inside creation. In other words, the decisions we make, stemming as they appear to do from inside ourselves as our responses to external situations, actually originate further inside than the inside of ourselves.

To witness the Origin, you must be prepared to go far inside yourself – then further still.

Conversely, the external situations which we encounter in the moment of decision are the product of an inexorable series of influences and events manifesting outwardly.

To know the Actor, you have to act in the world. Travel. Decide. Interact.

Allah says in the Qur'an, in the chapter of Fussilat 52:

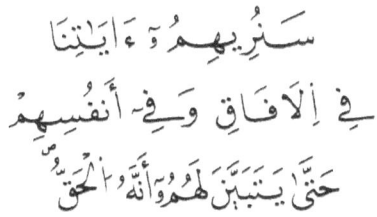

We will show them Our Signs on the horizon
and within themselves
until it is clear to them that it is the truth.

You can either decide you want this clarification of the truth to happen on agreeable terms – by taking the journey to Allah – or you can ignore it or resist it and have it happen to you on disagreeable terms. That is the meaning of the Garden and the Fire: the two opposite realities which every human spirit will go to, either one or the other.

WA ASH-HADU ANNA MUHAMMADAN RASULULLAH

After declaring in public that there is no god but Allah and divesting yourself of the idea of permanence, you affirm the trustworthy source and guide by testifying that Muhammad, may Allah bless him and grant him peace, is the Messenger of Reality.

Given the total and unequivocal power of the Creator, and that the overriding attribute of the Creator is Mercy, how could the Creator not bring forth somebody to guide you to Him? It is unthinkable that He would not. Note that we say 'He', because that is the pronoun He gives Himself, not because of gender or patriarchy, which are descriptors of the world.

The overriding attribute of the Creator is Mercy. Allah names Himself 'ar-Rahman' and 'ar-Raheem'. The former means merciful to everything, believing or not, animate or inanimate. The latter means merciful in a particular and additional way to those who believe in Him.

Allah is Merciful.

The Muslim begins everything by remembering this: "Bismillahi ar-Rahmani ar-Raheem". Muslims don't like to do anything without saying this. Before eating. Before driving. Before getting out of bed. Before setting pen to paper. Muslims say this to themselves throughout the day: "Bismillah". In the Name of Allah. "Bismillahi ar-Rahmani ar-Raheem". In the Name of Allah, All-Merciful, Most Merciful. Existence is fundamentally merciful and Muslims remind themselves of this all the time, even despite the harshnesses and hardships that may happen in oneself and with others. Events are part of that mercy and the pattern of the Messenger trains you to see that.

Allah says of the Messenger of Allah, may Allah bless him and grant him peace:

Qur'an, Al-Anbiya 106:

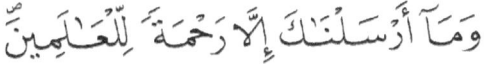

We have only sent you
as a mercy to all the worlds.

Not only is it part of His Mercy that He sent us the Messenger of Allah, Muhammad, may Allah bless him and grant him peace. The Messenger of Allah is the culmination and the highest aspect of His Mercy. Muslims call him the Best of Creation. There could be no greater gift than that which gives us access to Reality and how to live in accordance and harmony with it.

That is why the Messenger of Allah, may Allah bless him and grant him peace, came with the Shari'a of Islam. In the words of my Master, may Allah have mercy on him, this Shari'a is "a freely chosen social contract of believers who agree to live within its parameters."

Muhammad is the Messenger of Allah and he can only be approached through recognition of his true station, his true reality, which is that he was the perfect slave of Allah. His perfection was part of his 'design' and, as I said before, was not attained by him, although anything that can be achieved through man's efforts was achieved by him, and he was the best of people in both innate and learned characteristics.

Just as the predominant attribute of His Lord is mercy, so the predominant attribute of the Messenger was mercy, may Allah bless him and grant him peace.

To recognise him is to recognise this perfection as a human possibility – and your own possibility. Not of achieving the same level as him, which is impossible, but of attaining some of his blessings, a 'portion of Prophethood', the treasures readily available if you seek: if you are prepared to leave behind the encumbrances to which you have been so attached.

MUHAMMAD, THE MESSENGER OF ALLAH

So who is this man who emerged among the desert Arabs with a message for all of mankind until the end of the human situation?

Who is this man whose outer actions and condition we know from widespread reports and whose inner condition has been carried down the years to our time by face-to-face transmission?

What was he like?

His Companions, who belonged to a culture which valued eloquence and language above most other things, were careful to report and record everything they witnessed about him and these reports were kept. Vast amounts of highly detailed, widely verified descriptive material exists.

The great Andalusian scholar and judge Qadi 'Iyad gathered together what he considered to be the most important of these reports, along with his own thoughts and judgements on the matter, in a book known as 'Ash-Shifa', whose full Arabic title translates as: 'Healing by recognising what is due to the Chosen One'. It became acknowledged as the foremost statement written by man about the Messenger of Allah, may Allah bless him and grant him peace.

In it he says:

> Muhammad, may Allah bless him and grant him peace, was neither excessively tall nor short. Neither pale nor very dark, nor was his hair curly or completely straight. He passed away with no more than twenty white hairs on his head. He had a proportionate body: broad shouldered, with his hair generally reaching his shoulders, although on other occasions it reached his earlobes or the middle of his ears. He would let his hair hang over his forehead, but later he began to part it; he would comb his hair

and beard. He had a dense beard, a slight roundness to his face, and the pupils of his eyes were intensely black.

He had long eyelashes and a fine line of hair stretching from his chest to his navel. He walked with determination as if walking downhill.

The people of insight consider this way of walking a sign of intention, the opposite of which is doing things aimlessly. The people of discernment among the Muslims ask for Allah's forgiveness for doing anything without intention. He, may Allah bless him and grant him peace, said, "Actions are by intention." You could say that Islam is the science of intention, and that all your life's unfolding is a picture drawn by your intention.

His face would shine as if it were the moon.

This is the Arabs' way of describing the light of Iman. Iman is belief, which is accepting the true nature of existence. Light is the opposite of darkness. The dark face carries signs of the wrongs it has done. The light of Iman is the light of the opposite. It can be the result of the prayer, which leaves a physical mark on the forehead but, more profoundly, a spiritual impression on the physiognomy. The one who has prayed a lot looks different. It can be actions such as freely giving of one's wealth, visiting the sick or taking care of one's community. It can be gained by remembrance and contemplation of Allah in secret, in the depths of the night. And it can emerge in the face of the one who loves the Messenger and emulates whatever he can of his actions and states. And it can be given to someone by Allah without connection or cause.

A person's life is written in their face, which is why the Messenger of Allah, may Allah bless him and grant him peace, talked about the believer's ability to read faces.

He had a pleasant voice.

Qadi 'Iyad says that Umm Ma'bad, a Bedouin woman who gave him and his close companion hospitality on their migration to Madinah, described him thus:

> Sweet in speech, distinct, without using too few or too many words. It was as if his speech consisted of threaded pearls. He had a loud voice which was very melodious, may Allah bless him and grant him peace.

Qadi 'Iyad says that when he laughed, it was a smile, and that he did not show the back of his throat or throw his head back. It was what my Master used to call 'mirth'.

These and other aspects of his behaviour are matters of refinement, like his words, may Allah bless him and grant him peace, advising the Muslim to "supress the yawn". It doesn't mean don't yawn. It means certain bodily functions are best contained. For the one who contains yawning and laughter, it ennobles the character.

> His cheekbones did not protrude and his mouth was wide. His stomach and chest were the same width. He had a lot of hair on his shoulders, forearms and upper chest. He had long upper arms, wide palms and thick fingers. His heels were not fleshy. In between his shoulders was the seal of prophethood like the button of a curtain canopy or a pigeon's egg.

This curtain button is a simile particular to the Arabs. One could say a small pebble on the beach.

> When he walked, it was as if the earth folded up for him; the Companions would exert

themselves to keep up with him, while he would continue walking with ease.

His favourite clothing was the tunic or qamis, white garments and hibarah, which was a type of red-striped upper garment.

By his example, he gave his Companions and everyone who came after them permission to wear different kinds of clothing: sometimes plain, sometimes bright colours. He made things broad for his followers, both then and now, by not restricting himself to any particular colour or clothing.

The preferable clothing is the clothing of one's own culture, provided it covers the 'awra'. For men that means everything between the navel and the knees, and for women, everything except the face and hands. It is not adopting the clothing of another culture, such as Americans wearing Arab clothes. The Messenger of Allah did not come to spread Arab culture. He came to help people set aside what would not be good for them and embrace what would be good for them.

Much has been made of how Muslims, and Muslim women especially, are supposed to dress. It has been misleadingly presented as a matter of religious rights, religious identity or culture by people whose voices are allowed in the media.

What Allah orders is a degree of modesty. Every society has its degree of covering. The difference is that the Muslims' covering comes from a Prophetic source, while others cannot make this claim. Clothing or lack of it is not a punishable offence in Islam. But Allah does order us to cover ourselves. And exposing what has the potential to allure and excite the other sex is considered inappropriate, unwise and reprehensible.

> The Messenger of Allah's shirt sleeves would reach his wrist. On various occasions he wore a red-striped two-piece suit consisting of a waist-wrapper and a wrapper for the upper part of the body, a tight-sleeved and quilted double upper garment, a robe, a black turban whose two tails he let hang over his shoulders, and a wraparound made of animal hair. He would wear a ring, leather socks and sandals.
>
> Just as he was perfect in spiritual strength, he was perfect in physical strength, as numerous reports demonstrate. It is narrated that Rukanah was the strongest man in the Quraysh –

the dominant tribe of Makkah to which the

Messenger of Allah belonged

> – who, one day, happened to be alone with the Messenger of Allah on one of the mountain trails of Makkah, so the Messenger of Allah said to him, "Rukanah, aren't you afraid of Allah and don't you accept what I am inviting you to?" Rukanah replied, "If I knew it was true, I would follow you." The Messenger of Allah said, "Tell me, if I defeat you in wrestling, will you accept that what I am saying is true?" He replied, "Yes," so he, may Allah bless him and grant him peace, said, "Stand up then and let's wrestle." The Messenger of Allah grabbed him and threw him down, because Rukanah lost control over himself. Then he said, "Do it again, Muhammad," so he threw him over again twice, to which he replied, "This is incredible, you are actually throwing me down."

Rukanah returned to his people and accepted Islam, and won the Prophet's companionship.

Qadi 'Iyad continues:

> Allah purified him in spirit and body and kept him free from any faults and blemishes,

and gave him wisdom and judgement. Allah used him to open eyes that were blind, hearts that were covered and ears that were deaf, and He made people believe in him. Those to whom Allah had allotted a portion of the booty of happiness, honoured and helped him. Those for whom Allah had written wretchedness, rejected him and turned away from His signs.

If someone has been blessed with even one or two of the qualities of perfection and nobility – whether lineage, beauty, power, knowledge, forbearance, courage or generosity – he is considered noteworthy and people use him as an example. People's heart-felt esteem of these qualities makes people who have them honoured, long after they have died. So what then can be said of the worth of someone who possesses all of these qualities in such abundance that they cannot be counted or expressed in words? It would be impossible for him to have gained them either by graft or guile.

The way Allah had made our Prophet, may Allah bless him and grant him peace, is what caused and still causes people to believe in him and trust him.

This includes his innate attributes as well as perfect courtesy and manners, all of which draw people close and make them incline towards the one who has them.

> Anas said, "I have not smelled amber, musk or anything more fragrant than the smell of the Messenger of Allah, may Allah bless him and grant him peace."
>
> Ahmad ibn Hanbal and others related that the Prophet could see eleven stars in the Pleiades. This, according to Ahmad ibn Hanbal and others, refers to the total which it is physically possible to see with the naked eye. Clear-sightedness is one of the special traits of the Prophets and one of their qualities.

Another of his qualities was that when he turned to face someone, he would turn to face them directly.

> It is related that the Prophet said, "The kind of food which I prefer is that with many hands in it."

Muslims dislike eating alone, because the Prophet said, may Allah bless him and grant him peace, that

Shaytan – the one who incites to bad acts – eats with the solitary.

> Aisha said, "The Prophet, may Allah bless him and grant him peace, never filled his stomach completely. When he was with his family, he did not ask them for food nor desire it. If they fed it to him, he ate. He accepted whatever they served him and he drank whatever they gave him to drink."

He, may Allah bless him and grant him peace, used to say that we should fill a third of our stomachs with food and a third with drink, and leave a third unfilled. And when asked when one should eat, he replied, "When you are hungry."

My Master, may Allah have mercy on him, wrote about the Messenger:

> His name means the Praiseworthy.
> Muhammad, may Allah bless him and grant him peace, was forbearing, honest, just and chaste. His hand never touched the hand of a woman over whom he did not

have rights, with whom he did not have sexual relations, or who was not lawful for him to marry. He was the most generous of men.

Neither a dinar nor a dirham was left him in the evening. If anything remained and there was no one to give it to, night having fallen suddenly, he would not retire to his apartment until he was able to give this excess to whoever needed it. He was never asked for anything but that he gave it to the asker. He would prefer the seeker to himself and his family, so his store of grain for the year was often used up before the end of the year. He patched his sandals and clothing, did household chores and ate with his women-folk. He was shy (– i.e. modest –) and would not stare into people's faces. He answered the invitation of the slave and the free-born and he accepted presents even if they consisted merely of a draught of milk or a rabbit's leg, while because of hunger he would at times tie two stones around his stomach.

He ate what was at hand and did not refrain from any permitted food. He did not eat reclining. He attended feasts, visited the sick, attended funerals and walked among his enemies without a guard. He was the humblest of men, the most silent without being insolent and the most eloquent without being lengthy. He was always joyful and never awed by the affairs of this world. He rode a horse, a male camel, a mule, an ass, he walked barefoot and bareheaded at different times.

He loved perfumes and disliked foul smells.

He sat and ate with the poor.

He tyrannised nobody and accepted the excuse of the one who begged his pardon.

He joked, but he only spoke the truth. He laughed but did not burst out laughing. He did not eat better food or wear better clothes than his servants.

The conduct of this perfect ruler was untaught. He could neither read nor write, he grew up with shepherds in an ignorant desert land and was an orphan without father or mother. He refused to curse his enemy saying, "I was sent to forgive, not to curse." When asked to wish evil on anyone, he blessed them instead.

Anas ibn Malik, his servant, said: "He

never said to me about anything of which he disapproved, 'Why did you do it?' Moreover, his wives would not rebuke me without his saying, 'Let it be. It was meant to happen.'"

If there was a bed, he slept on it, if not he reclined on the earth. He was always the first to extend a greeting. In a handshake he was never the first to release his hand. He preferred his guest over himself and would offer the cushion on which he reclined until it was accepted. He called his companions by their kunya (byname) so as to show honour to them, and the children so as to soften their hearts. One did not argue in his presence. He only spoke the truth. He was the most smiling and laughing of men in the presence of his Companions, admiring what they said and mingling with them. He never found fault with his food. If he was pleased with it he ate it and if he disliked it he left it. If he disliked it he did not make it hateful to someone else. He did not eat very hot food, and he ate what was in front of him on the plate, within his reach, eating with three fingers. He wiped the dish clean with his fingers saying, "The last morsel is very blessed." He did not wash his hands until he had licked them clean of food. He quaffed milk but sipped water.

Sayyiduna 'Ali, his closest Companion, said: "Of all men he was the most generous, the most open hearted, the most truthful, the most fulfilling of promise, the gentlest of temper, and the noblest towards his family. Whoever saw him unexpectedly was awed by him, and whoever was his intimate loved him."

This is a very small portion of the things we know about him, may Allah bless him and grant him peace, pertaining to his outer description and character. But he was also perfect in his inner states, which have also been transmitted down to us, more of which later.

FIVE PILLARS

Man is a worshipping creature and a ritual creature. If you take that away from him, he will still do it, but in perverse and negative ways.

To understand this, you may have to jettison ideas you have of worship. People go wrong in two basic ways: too much emphasis on forms, and rejection of forms. Too much emphasis on form means thinking about worship as excessively ritualistic and being obsessed with minutiae, to the point where it is believed that you are saved by the worship itself, or the ritual, or by doing the ritual 'right', rather than it being a means to something.

Rejection of form means saying that it is the

principle that matters, or that just believing something is enough and actions are unimportant, or saying that what is inside is what matters and what is on the outside doesn't matter, especially particular forms of worship.

The Muslim acknowledges the means, the forms and the rituals and admits of their necessity, while knowing that none of it has any meaning unless imbued with some degree of intention, obedience and wanting.

SHAHADA

The first of Islam's five pillars is the declaration already discussed. When you enter Islam by saying in front of witnesses that there is no god except Allah and that Muhammad is the Messenger of Allah, you also undertake, in front of those same witnesses, to do every one of the five prayers every day until you die, to fast from first light to sunset in every month of Ramadan, to go to the House of Allah in Makkah at least once in your life if you are able, and to give away one fortieth of your excess wealth each year, if it rises above a certain amount and stays above it for a year.

These are the core things that are demanded of

you by your Creator. They are what will keep you straight in your humanity. Allah would not have made them mandatory had they not been what we need.

Every human creature tends towards these worship-elements. If the Prophetically given forms are not there, humanly invented forms take their place, whether consciously or not, because the human creature has the inclination of worship built into it.

My Master, may Allah have mercy on him, used to say that each Pillar can be thought of as a tax given by the slave to the Lord.

The Shahada is what you pay, what you give up of your intellectual sovereignty, because by saying it publicly, you state something that is not from you and not about you. You become like the Companions who, when asked about a thing by the Messenger, would reply, "Allah and His Messenger know best." It is freedom from the shackles and the knot of the self which you yourself can never untie.

PRAYER

The Prayer is a tax on your time. Blessed is he who pays this tax. As the prayer's time comes upon you,

you have to stop and do it. It is turning away from the world. You turn to face Qibla, which is the direction of the House of Allah in Makkah from wherever you are. Whatever you are oriented towards at that moment, you turn away from it. The prayer begins with the 'takbir': the hands are raised to either side of the head – the seat of preoccupation – and cast down, casting away the affairs of the world, and you say, "Allahu akbar" – Allah is greater. Then you recite from the Qur'an, something short or something not so short, then you bow, bending at the hips, then you stand again, then you go down and prostrate with your forehead on the ground. At last, the heart is above the head and the slave is doing with the body what that body was made to do, physicalising the submission which it has longed to make but has been making to this thing or that thing, to this idea or that idea.

This prayer, five times in the rhythm of the rising, moving and setting of the sun, renders the crack in the edifice of the proposition known as 'you'. The proposition of being the owner and the master of yourself. The proposition of being dominated by yourself – or somebody else. When the hands are cast down and the head goes onto the floor, it is all left behind.

After prostrating, the slave sits, then prostrates

again, in each position saying words which the Messenger taught his Companions. With that the slave has completed a cycle, called a 'rakat'. He stands and starts over. At first light you do two rakats, when the sun has passed the zenith you pray four, when it has passed half way down you pray four, when it has set you pray three, and when the light leaves the sky you pray four.

These five prayers become the waymarks of the day's cycle around which the activities of life coalesce and settle. If something impedes you, you make the prayer up when you next can. But if something seeks to stop it happening altogether, that something is your enemy, whether it is inside you or outside. Now you know who your enemies are. You have submitted to the Creator of the inward and the outward, so you will see who and what is your true friend and who and what is not.

The obligatory prayer is done not as a choice or when you feel moved or able, as in the collapsed religions. But neither does anyone force you to do it. It is self-chosen. It is an obligation you take upon yourself, given to you as a gift by Allah.

Before doing it, you purify yourself by washing your hands, mouth, nose, face, arms, ears, head and feet – briskly by rubbing with water. This waking-up or cooling down of the senses cleans off the murk of preoccupation and wipes away the turbidity of everything that happened since the last cycle of purification and prayer. It is a clean sheet.

Human creatures who do not have this will engage in something in its place: rituals, self-chosen, to fulfil and assuage the deep human need to express reverence and gratitude. Without Prophetic guidance, they will fall short, since Divine Prophecy is part of the human design and humans are incomplete without it. For those without it, their prayer-surrogate can even be whatever habits they set up to mark the points in the day.

The human creatures who do not have this are not tethered in time and place to Reality. Self-chosen rituals and habits still contain an element of self. They are not tethered.

Doing the prayer brings you in harmony with the creation of which you are part. It synchronises you with the movement of the sun in the sky and orientates you to a definite place on earth. Neither the sun, nor that place of worship, nor the direction are divine or worshipped. They are the divinely given frame of worship.

The prayer has physical, psychological and material benefits, although it is not done for those reasons. It is done out of obedience.

FASTING

Fasting the month of Ramadan is, in its simplest meaning, a tax on your eating and drinking, that most elemental of human needs. Since birth you have called out for food. As you enter adulthood and the feeding process becomes fixed, as if it were your 'right', you take on fasting. And you begin to escape the prison of false need.

But the core of fasting is not about not eating or being hungry, even if you do get hungry towards the end of the day. It is about delaying consumption and realising you didn't need it the way you thought. The freedom gained by fasting the obligatory fast is freedom from the infantile compulsion of 'putting-into-the-mouth'. Smoking is also disallowed during the day, as is the ingestion of anything at all. All that ritual and craving that has built up around eating, sucking and inhaling is set aside.

Fasting is done together with other Muslims and breaking the fast is done together. The sweetness and joy of the first bite when the sun sets is a shared joy. Love grows between the fasters.

Once darkness descends, you can eat, drink and have sexual relations. You can do everything in Ramadan which you do the rest of the time, except the timing is turned upside down. You stay up more at night and do extra prayers. You sleep or nap more in the day. You eat in the darkness instead of the daytime. It is a reversal. It is jettisoning the accretions of the year. It is purification, including for the digestion, the brain, the cells – and the spirit. It sublimates the mud structure of the personality which is built from infancy around food, drink and intimacy and how you get them. You still get them, but you cleanse and understand your relation to them.

ZAKAT

Zakat, the wealth tax. From the first moment you accrue wealth over and above your immediate needs, and then a year passes over that excess wealth, the poor have a right to some of it. One fortieth. The poor of a Muslim community have an incontestable right to a share of the excess wealth of its affluent members. Excess wealth is defined as 20 gold dinars, which is about 85 grams of gold, which at the time of writing is somewhere around $5500, of which you must pay 2.5%. On the level of today's taxation, zakat is miniscule. But anyone who tries to circumvent it is wilfully negating one of the Five Pillars of their own life-transaction. So, in a community or society in which many or most people strive in different degrees to be Muslim, this money flows automatically. Not only that, but it is a duty of the leader to forcibly extract payment from any individual, group or municipality who refuses to pay Zakat on openly evident wealth such as crops or livestock from productive land. Conversely, there are no powers to investigate hidden wealth, including cash. Hidden savings are the responsibility of their owner, unless that person's wealth is so much on display that it compels the leadership of the society to act.

Thus, as in all the legal measures of Islam, it is a dynamic between the authority and the individual and exists within a zone of other factors. The cutting off of the hand of the thief which the humanist media so love to be voyeuristically shocked about is first preceded by questions: does the one who took the property have enough to eat for three days in their house? If not, there is no punishment. In other words: what is wrong that the society allows someone to be without enough food? Legally, he is permitted to help himself – and Allah knows his real intentions. Secondly, was the property hidden away or was it on display? If on display, there is no punishment. The thief has to have gone into a closed house or building, having enough provisions at home to live on, and then steal something worth a significant amount (petty theft is not punished by cutting off the hand). And that, in a community or country with openly Muslim leadership and consisting wholly or mostly of Muslims. This and other laws are not enforced in other jurisdictions.

Anyone who has spent time in a Muslim country living with its people will know that it is virtually impossible to go hungry there, since it is the habit of people to feed you at all times, put you up in their houses and give generous gifts. Open generosity is a social norm, due to that being the practice of the Messenger and his Companions, and due to the people being closer to their nature through worship. 'Umar ibn al-Khattab, the second Ruler of Islam after the death of the Prophet, and one of his closest Companions, when he heard that a family in the city under his authority was going hungry, sat down and wept.

In other words, if in a functioning Muslim community with openly Muslim leadership someone still insists of stealing, despite there being no need, and invades someone's property to do so – and is witnessed in the act by two adult male witnesses (any less and there is no punishment) – then yes, in that exceedingly rare and flagrant case of badness, his hand is cut off. He is then left with that to live with, and people will take note of something very unambiguous. What does not happen is that the perpetrator is sent to languish in a prison together with other questionable people to become even worse than he already is.

Zakat, the poor-tax, is the magnificent peak of a vast mountain range of charitable practice in which the Muslims engage in direct emulation of their Prophet and his Companions, and in harmony with their natural humanity. The Messenger of Allah was the most generous man among a generous people for whom giving liberally was a matter of pride. Qadi 'Iyad in his book about the Prophet says:

> Examine the biography of our Prophet and his character in dealing with wealth. You will find that he was given the treasures of the earth and the keys to the lands. Booty, which had not been lawful for any prophet before him, was allowed to him. During his lifetime, he conquered the Hijaz, the Yemen and all of the Arabian Peninsula, as well as the areas bordering Syria and Iraq. He was brought a fifth of the booty as well as the jizya-tax and zakat-tax of which earlier kings had only obtained a fraction. He

was given gifts by several foreign kings. He did not keep any of this for himself nor withhold a single dirham of it. He spent it all via its proper channels, enriched others with it and strengthened the Muslims by it.

He said, "I do not feel easy if any gold dinar remains with me overnight, except for a dinar which I have set aside to pay a debt."

Sometimes he was given dinars and divided them and perhaps six would be left over. Then he would give them to some of his wives. He would not sleep until he had divided them out. Then he would say, "Now I can rest." When he died, his armour was in pawn to feed his family.

Not only that. Pay close attention, because this is very important, especially today: the Messenger of Allah, may Allah bless him and grant him peace, made his date orchard in Madinah al-Munawwara into a waqf to assist in the protection of Islam. What is a waqf and why is it important? It meant his orchard was no longer his property in the same sense as before. Its legal status changed so that its usufruct was for the designated cause. The income it generated, after paying for its own maintenance and management, went to that cause. He made another orchard in Fadak into a waqf for travellers. The income this generated was given to them for their needs. 'Umar ibn al-Khattab, may Allah be pleased with him, set up a waqf for war veterans and to assist slaves in buying their freedom. This became the practice of Muslims from that point on, and grew to become what you might call the social welfare system of Islam, although strictly speaking it is not a system, since there is no structural compulsion, nor any centralised control. It is closer to an organic pattern spread by emulation. Some centuries later things had reached the point that around a third of the lands of the Osmanli Dawlet (incorrectly named the Ottoman Empire) consisted of such waqfs, including the whole of Palestine, whose income, after paying for its own maintenance, was set aside to maintain the Sacred Precincts of Makkah and Madinah in Arabia.

Waqfs were dedicated to every social need. Education, healthcare, the poor, road repairs, helping people who had fallen on various kinds of hardship. Even feeding the birds in winter. The list is endless and it is one of the largely forgotten facts of history that nations took care of themselves this way. Crucially, it means that in a functioning Muslim society, social welfare is run on totally different lines. By the emulation of Prophetic practice, waqf becomes commonplace and those renting such a waqf, or spending into that property, know that by doing so, they are benefiting their society, while receiving no less benefit themselves. Compare this with the system put forward as 'modern' by the dominant nexus today, in which moneylenders (banks) have insinuated themselves as a parasitic component into almost every transaction and every property ownership and every rental, and in which governments tax their citizens, taking everything in centrally and then distributing it in a machine-like grid with the invasive financial surveillance and lack of privacy that entails.

All this relates to Zakat inasmuch as Zakat is the pinnacle of the mountain range of Muslim giving-practice. Zakat is the highest pillar of natural giving and financial flow that you need to rediscover if you wish to help mankind. It is not a system that can be applied from outside like some kind of divine social engineering project. It can only come from believing people who recognise the Prophet and emulate him, and especially through leaders who love him and emulate him, seeking Allah's favour. This emulation of Prophetic financial practice, alas, is lacking among most leaders at the time of writing. It remains for people of courage and ability to become Muslim, or awaken to the Islam they already have, and take on this sublime endeavour.

In inward terms, Zakat is also a tax on man's perception of himself as self-sustaining. He thinks he has wealth and that it makes him secure. The taking of the fortieth is a protection against this idea becoming entrenched, making an idol out of the wealth and the self that owns it.

Allah says in His Noble Book:

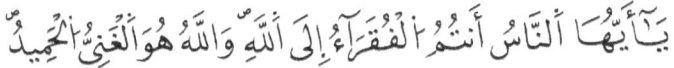

> Mankind! you are the poor in need of Allah
> whereas Allah is the Rich Beyond Need,
> the Praiseworthy.

HAJJ

The Hajj is the pilgrimage to Makkah. It was done by the Prophet and his Companions. It is also an ancient rite from before Islam. It encompasses the human need for ritual gathering and travel.

You must do it.

You could say it is the tax you pay on your life. Why? You go not knowing whether you will return.

You straighten your affairs and make or update any will you have. For most of the world's Muslims, it is the biggest and most expensive journey they will ever undertake. The prayer marks the rhythm of the day and week, Ramadan and Zakat the cycle of the month and year. The Hajj is a cycle of one lifetime. It is singular. It has to be done once only, by those who are financially and physically able.

Hajj is about intention. None of the acts of worship are valid without intention, but it is on Hajj where this becomes most apparent. In former times, most pilgrims would face considerable physical danger from banditry, illness and the sheer length of the journey. A Hajji might not return for many months. These difficulties barely exist now, but in their place are the difficulties of our age: excessive cost, obstructive bureaucracy, overcrowding, and the state of semi-bondage most of mankind find themselves in due to the dominant forms of salaried work and debt-based financial arrangements.

Whatever obstructs you in completing any and each of the Five Pillars is identifiable as the particular enemy-form that belongs to your circumstances and the age in which you live.

As you near Makkah and cross one of the waymarks that delineate its outermost region, you do the ritual wash and, for men, replace your usual clothing with two white cloths. These are similar to, or may indeed be, the cloths you will be wrapped in when you are buried.

You arrive in the Sacred Precinct. You enter the Mosque of Makkah. You set eyes on the House of Allah, that cubic building draped in black whose significance is not what is in it (nothing) but that it is the orientation point, the focus for the waves of prayer that continue day and night as the earth rotates.

Shaykh Abdalhaqq Bewley writes in his book 'Islam – the Natural Form of Man':

> The Hajj is unique. There is nothing that happens on our planet that is in any way comparable to it. It represents the only truly global pattern of human social behaviour. If someone out in space were to observe the surface of the earth as a whole over a period of years, indeed of centuries, they would see many localised patterns of movement by human beings. They would see cities filling up and emptying out on a daily basis as people go to and from their places of work. They would probably notice within the continent of Europe a seasonal movement backwards and forwards between

North and South as people head for the sun for their summer holidays. But in the main, the movement of people about the surface of the earth would appear to be completely random to an outside observer and it would seem that there was no real cohesive human activity involving the whole human race.

Just one thing would belie this conclusion. At a certain time every year people would start, at first by ones and twos and gradually in ever increasing numbers, to move towards and gather together in one particular arid spot on the earth's surface. If the observer had very sophisticated equipment he would see the growing gathering going round and round in circles about one central point and then backwards and forwards between two adjacent points. Then on a clearly pre-specified date connected to the lunar year, the whole mass of gathered people would be seen to move into a nearby valley and the following day to stream across the desert and remain stationary there for several hours.

They would then return to the valley from which they had set out and, after a couple of days, they would start to disperse and return to all the places, near and far, from which they had originally come. Our observer in space would certainly conclude that this was the one discernable phenomenon which tied together the whole human race and the only global pattern of human activity.

One could add the Prayer, the Fast and the Zakat to that, were the observer able to see things in such intimacy. The prayer is a wave of bowing and prostrating bodies travelling in a vast ripple around the rotating globe as the sun's light moves across its surface.

The Fast is the cessation of eating on the sun-facing half of the world for every day of one month of each lunar year. The zakat is an annual movement of valuable possessions to central points (leaders and their collectors) and out to other points (recipients): a breathing lung of wealth.

Hajj. Arriving at the House of Allah is arriving at the heart of yourself. Everything of your life revolves around your heart. My Master said that the heart is like a magnet: whatever it wants, it draws towards it.

You circle the house of Allah amid the tumult of all humanity. Every form of humanity is there.

You cling to the door of the House of Allah and beg your Lord for your heart's desire. You kiss the Black Stone embedded in one of its corners, because our Prophet kissed it, may Allah bless him and grant him peace. Therein lies the root of how Islam works: we copy him in something which may or may not appear to have outward utility, and in doing so we are taught. It is not magic or a mystery, although not everyone knows about it. One of the great Companions, 'Abdullah ibn 'Umar, was seen making his camel turn round in a particular place and was asked why. He said, "I don't know. I once saw the Messenger of Allah doing it, so I do it." So it is with the Hajj. It is beyond reason. And its gifts are countless.

After circling the House, you go to the Maqam of Ibrahim, the place where Ibrahim used to stand, peace be upon him. You prostrate there amid the crowds. You then go to Safa, a nearby hillock. You face the House of Allah and ask Allah for what you want. You hurry to another nearby rocky hillock, Marwa. Again you ask Allah. You go back to Safa. You ask Allah. You hurry back to Marwa. You ask Allah. You jog back and forth, crossing the well of Zamzam, whose water sprung up in the time of Ibrahim in response to the need of his slave-woman, Hajjar, and their blessed baby son Ismail.

Then, when a particular day of the lunar month arrives, you walk or ride many miles to Arafat, a plain outside Makkah. You stand there with the millions of Hajjis, tired, dishevelled, hot, dusty, sore. This is the core of what you came for, because of all the rites of Hajj, this is the one which, if you fail to do it, you have no Hajj. The Messenger said, "Hajj is Arafat."

There on Arafat you have nothing at all. All you have is time with your Lord. So you have everything. Away from every utility and every circumstance of your worldly existence, your hands are on the very levers of your life as you stand, asking Reality for whatever it is which arises in your heart – for yourself, for others.

You are now gathered together with millions of your fellow men and women. The Last Day is brought near: the day on which all of the human creatures who ever lived will be gathered again. Modern cynicism towards the Resurrection is not in fact modern. It is age-old. There will always be those who refuse to accept that we can be brought back. Allah says, referring to the mankind's resurrection:

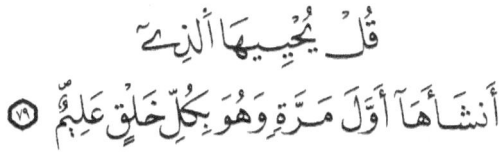

> Say 'He who made them in the first place
> will bring them back to life.
> He has total knowledge of each created thing'

He Who made you in the first place will bring you back to life. Therefore, denying the possibility of the Resurrection is like denying our being here in the first place. What is so unbelievable about being brought back to life, given that we came to exist in the first place?

While many of mankind stream to their sports stadiums in clamouring droves, engaging in its rituals of gathering and spending, drinking, shouting at athletes whose hourly earnings equal a lifetime's toil for most men, the Muslims on Hajj find existential relief and Divine openings in a rite which has existed since the dawn of man.

The Hajjis leave the plain of Arafat at sunset. As they stream back through the narrow valley of Muzdalifa, resting for a time on the way, before heading for the final rites of Hajj, they realise it was for THIS gathering, not those other worldly ones, that the urge to gather was set inside their hearts. The urge to congregate. To move from a place to a place in crowds. To amass. To experience a togetherness that cannot be known except to those who have partaken in it.

The end of Hajj is marked by the Great 'Eid, which Muslims celebrate all over the world. Every people has its 'Eid. Consider New Year's Eve: the humanist, capitalist, surrogate 'Eid, based not on following any Prophet but on the ticking of the clock and the advancing of the years, a chronological festival for a world system based on numbers, celebrated by obliteration of the senses and an already-failed resolution to be better – the materialist clean sheet.

Not so the Muslim, who comes back from Hajj or from the Eid, renewed.

The true clean slate.

IDOLS

'Tawhid' is to affirm the Oneness of Allah. 'Shirk' is its opposite and is often translated as idolatry, but it isn't just men bowing to carved forms. It can be much more sophisticated than that. Different times bring forth different idols. They can be forms set up to worship physically, like immediately before Islam and in religions like Hinduism, whereby divine power is attributed to entities or ideas claimed to be or to represent gods. At other times this divinity is invested in particular people, such as in the time of Pharaoh, and at stages in history when peoples have attributed godlike status to their leaders, either openly and outright, like the Japanese emperors, or by implication, like recent communist dictators. And, significantly, in wrongly attributing divine status to legitimate prophets, more of which later.

In this time of ours, minds scoff at such primitivism. But they commit the very same act by investing divine attributes in conceptual abstractions.

What people wrongly worship today, meaning they ascribe independent power to it, are ideologies that lead to particular actions. Inventions of the human mind are thought to be sacred and people believe them to exist as eternal principles innate in the very fabric of humanity.

And people fear evil idols. People who have lost hold of the rope of the Divine live in inordinate fear of particular things. Further back in Christian history it was, among other things, the Church itself. The institution and its priests became idols which were said to – and thus in a perverted way did – hold sway over people's destinies. People feared excommunication as if it were damnation itself. It was as if the priests and the Pope were the ones actually standing in judgment over men, and membership of the Church were salvation itself. And people said – and still say – that it was the church itself which made particular people into saints by the bizarre administrative ritual of canonisation.

This is what the Muslims call 'shirk'. It means giving things or concepts a share in what rightly belongs to Allah. The Qur'anic word 'shirk' comes from the word for partner. It is putting what is other-than-Allah in a false partnership with Allah. It does not have to be the open declaration that a thing is a god.

The Messenger of Allah, may Allah bless him and grant him peace, said, "Oh Allah, we seek refuge in You from associating anything with You knowingly, and we ask Your forgiveness for doing so unknowingly."

Inordinate, misplaced fear or adulation of things and ideas suggests hidden shirk.

The idol of Superior Race, recently ascendant in the age of racial colonialism, is now largely discredited. It seems absurd today that Hitler declared his incoherent book to be 'the book for all Germans for all time' and claimed the Third Reich would last a thousand years.

Closely tied to the idol of race is the idol of Empire. While claiming itself to be a Christian – and White – undertaking, the British Empire became an idolatrous overreach. People believed it was something final or absolute. Highly intelligent and gifted people dedicated themselves to it with enormous energy and enthusiasm.

The nineteenth and twentieth centuries saw the rise of new, abstract gods, most especially 'Progress', which has since morphed into the 'Growth' which societies are now supposed to be incapable of surviving without. Growth is a mantra and its espousal bears the attributes of a religion. Its pursuit is a perverted worship.

Also emergent in the early twentieth century was 'the Self' in the sense of individualism. One of the many rituals of this god is advertising, which tells you to feed the existence of your individuality and personal needs, encouraged by phrases such as 'you deserve it' and 'believe in yourself'.

The bitter irony is that people know individualism is a subterfuge for selling things and making a small and shrinking number of people very rich. But it continues. Nobody quite believes in false gods, but they still act in the play.

As a Muslim you have the tools to rise above this. The axe with which to fell these ideological gods is the act of putting your head on the ground for the One Who does not come to an end, and the act of establishing the limits set out by legitimate Divine Revelation. In this age of ours, this means, above all, the limits Allah places on the nature of financial transactions, since that is where the dominant society has gone most wrong and where its biggest idols lie – more of which later.

As mankind moved into the twenty-first century, new things were held up that were supposed to have absolute reality. People now have nightmares about 'Climate Change'. This is not to say that the destruction of large swathes of the environment is not true. It is. The foul offspring of the god of Progress. But a religion is made out of fighting it.

Then there was the recent 'Covid'. This short-lived idol we were supposed to obey was backed by another false god, 'Science'. Nothing is allowed to be true except if approved by Science. We are told to 'follow the science' as if it were some kind of entity with independent existence, instead of a description of a useful yet innately conflictual and shifting zone of ideas and experiments. People are 'cancelled' (= excommunicated) if they disobey Science, or rather if they do not follow a particular science wielded as a tool for very particular political, social and financial ends.

Many brilliant people who have dedicated their lives to good works have been excommunicated and exiled out of public life by confronting the idol of Science.

Idolatry mixes truth with untruth. Covid is indeed an unusual disease by which means people do meet their ends, especially the old and weak. But it was made into more than that and as with all idols, it became a means to test the limits of power, exert influence and divert money streams.

As one examines these modern gods one by one, the biggest emerge. One is 'the Market'. It and Growth are by-products of the practice of 'riba', whose limits were laid out and clarified in no uncertain terms by the coming of Islam, even though many of them had in fact already long been known. These limits are nothing other than financial-rightness-in-action. This too I will discuss later.

Another false god is 'Democracy', which is that people pretend to be ruled by people whom they despise, and who mostly have no expertise in good leadership and no expertise in the fields they are supposed to hold ministerial or departmental authority over. Instead they have ambition and a pronounced sense of opportunity, shrewdness, a willingness to embrace self-promotion and the habit of mingling truth with lies. People think they choose them in the ritual of voting, while grumbling that it is all despicable. Democracy is an idol. No serious discourse about politics or power is permitted without it. To deny it is to risk excommunication.

HUMAN RIGHTS

The majority is not always right. Allah says in His Noble Book:

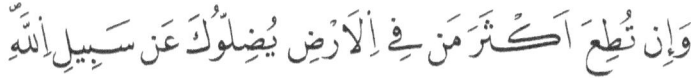

If you obeyed most of those on earth,
they would misguide you from Allah's Way.

Sadly for the whole of mankind, the Muslims have not been immune to the allure of some of these idols. 'Human Rights' is a good example. This set of supposed moral principles is now widely considered to be somehow intrinsic to mankind's very fabric. Its absolutism is such, and its promotion so absolute, that Muslim 'reformers', cowed after military defeat and conquest and with hearts inclined towards their conquerors, have sought to 'Islamise' Human Rights by an agonised contortion, looking into the sources of Islam to see what might comply or be twisted to fit in with this imported belief system. They and their successors have cobbled together pronouncements that Islam is indeed compatible with Human Rights and even an upstanding upholder of them. But what this really means is changing Islam, because although Allah does indeed give rights to different categories of people, Islam is not based on rights. It is based on responsibilities. It protects rights in an utterly different way and always as a consequence of the Muslims' responsibility towards their fellow humans and towards their Lord.

But institutions now exist such as an Islamic Human Rights Commission, and statements and positions are put out by Muslim leaders based on Human Rights. For example, in 2022, Nupur Sharma, the national spokeswoman of India's Hindu ruling party, publicly insulted the Messenger of Allah on television, may Allah bless him and grant him peace and may Allah protect him and give people knowledge of his true stature. In response to this base act, which reveals the utter worthlessness and darkness of the person who did it, Qatar's Foreign Ministry issued a statement saying, "Allowing such Islamophobic remarks to continue without punishment, constitutes a grave danger to the protection of human rights and may lead to further prejudice and marginalisation."

This is not the language of Islam. The Messenger of Allah is the best of mankind and has been put beyond reproach by Allah in the Qur'an. This statement of theirs (even if made for reasons of political expedience), by basing itself on the doctrine of Human Rights, gives the impression that the Muslims measure things by the same measure as humanists. The doctrine of Human Rights was concocted by indignant and rebellious men in response to the iniquities of late-stage Christian monarchical despotism in the 18th and 19th centuries. It became firmly established internationally after the two humanist World Slaughters.

No supposedly inalienable doctrine can be dressed up in Islamic clothing and passed off as Islam. To do so obscures Islam. Rather, justice in Islam is achieved by following, to the best of one's knowledge and ability, the rulings of Allah and His Messenger, may Allah bless him and grant him peace, under the authority of legitimate, open and accepted leadership (not in a power vacuum, under hidden leaders, or as vigilantism) and in the knowledge that Allah is the Knower of the Seen and the Unseen and that ultimate justice belongs to Him. In return for making such judgments with that intention, the one doing the judging is rewarded by Allah once if he judges wrongly and twice if he judges rightly. In Islam, the wronger and the wronged are understood to move within the Decree of Allah, may He be exalted. Far from absolving Muslims of the need to respond with justice, this understanding of the Decree frees them to be clear about their intentions in judging, fearing the consequences in their innermost selves and not fearing men, and confident in the knowledge that their hearts are ultimately seen and the outcome of every affair is ultimately known.

Note the flagrant hypocrisy of the foremost advocates of the doctrine of Human Rights, such as successive governments of the United States, France and the United Kingdom. Guantanamo Bay is the distillation and essence of non-rights, and the behaviour of American military personnel in its imperialistic conflicts, supported by their lackeys the British, has not afforded rights to the hundreds of thousands of bombed, napalmed and displaced humans. They themselves, in their books and films, are the most eloquent narrators of these crimes. The bastard son of the idol of Human Rights – which it likes to disown – is unjust war. The doctrine is false and has no legitimacy.

Since humanists believe in this doctrine's absolute authority, it can be said that they worship what originated it. What originated it is man himself. Humanism is worship of the human creature, since it ascribes absolute authority to man. Allah says in Surat al-Hajj:

> They worship besides Allah
> something for which
> no authority has come down.

Because false gods are against nature, they produce unnatural outcomes. 'Progress' has produced spiritually regressive human societies whose adults behave like children and have no sense of any higher purpose at all – isolated individuals without communities, who don't know who they are or what they are here for.

As for the false god of the Self, it has produced widespread suicide (which it says is people's 'right') and endemic depression.

The Market is another idol. According to the economists themselves, the term is merely a euphemism for a tiny number of people engaged in gambling and speculation. Their actions bleed and destroy livelihoods and countries. Their desire is that less and less people should have access to genuine trade and tangible, beneficial economic activity, so that their own wealth can grow. Whole governments fall in a day because of the Market.

With every emergency we are told we are in, titanic businesses and financial entities, owned by individuals and tiny groups of people – often unknown – grow richer, while small, productive businesses die. And the number of people owning half the wealth of the world shrinks. And we are told it is because of the Market.

Allah says of Ibrahim in Surat al-Anbiya:

He broke them in pieces

– meaning he broke the idols. Modern false gods are concepts and ideas by which people enrich themselves. The smashing of idols has to involve the deconstructing of those concepts and ideas.

Behind these idols are even more exacting false gods. One is 'Reason' itself. Some Muslims have felt compelled to insist that Islam is based on Reason, whereas it is in fact based on believing in and obeying Allah and His Messenger, may Allah bless him and grant him peace. Belief is not encompassed by the faculty of reason. Rather, men use the faculty of reason to enact what they believe in. If what they believe is legitimate, they will put reason to good use. If they believe in a lie, they will use reason to advance that lie.

The idolatry of this age is to ascribe to man himself a degree of power and authority to which he has no right. It is to place man up high as the ultimate arbiter of human affairs. God is thereby relegated to a relative concept. But it is us and all of creation who are relative. He, glory be to Him, is high above any ascription or relativisation.

Allah says in Surat an-Naml:

May Allah be exalted
above what they associate with Him.

THE IDOL OF INFINITE TIME

Think about the idol of time posited as absolute and infinite. In fact, time is created, just as the spatial dimensions are created. The content which fills time and space is created. Time has a beginning and an end.

Allah is that which has no beginning and no

end. Allah says:

$$\text{هُوَ الْأَوَّلُ وَالْآخِرُ}$$

He is the First and the Last.

In other words, Allah is before the beginning of time with a beforeness that is not chronological. He is after the end of time with a finality that is not chronological. It is He Who created time. Why is this so important? Because the false idol of infinite time is connected with the idol of Progress. The theory of evolution – which is no longer treated as a theory but as indisputable fact – is not objectionable for the reasons for which religious people are told they object to it. Whether Allah created the content of the universe suddenly or by means of a gradual process is not what is at issue. The lie implied by evolution is that everything is constantly getting better. The doctrine we live under, and which justifies and validates the practices of the enemies of nature, is that we have evolved and risen up out of the darkness of the past, most recently throwing off the shackles of 'primitive' religion and outdated forms of social organisation.

Allah says in Surat Al-An'am 26:

> Those who are kafir say,
> 'This is nothing but the myths of
> previous peoples.'

Man has an inbuilt tendency to avoid confrontation with Divine Instruction by abnegating the past. There is nothing new about this. The casting-away of things gone by is an essential doctrine of kufr, because it veils people from the Prophetic guidelines which are the only enactable resource upon which to base a natural society.

In the words of my Master, may Allah reward him:

> A version of reality has been instituted which accords with the power élite's programmes of the expropriation of personal wealth, and its relocation in inter-connected corporate and statal structures. To further hide the venal truth of this oligarchy it has proved propitious to borrow the evaluations and vocabulary of the emergent scientific method of materialist evolutionism. [...]
>
> The orthodoxy of the oligarchs divides history into two epochs [...].
>
> The first stage of history (from this

viewpoint) was the natural and 'primitive' society. From the moral point of view, everything about it was dreadful. It was presented as static. Its dominant condition was inescapable poverty for 'the people'. It was controlled and dictated to by hereditary rulers, kings and princes. They were by definition – that is, as princes and rulers – tyrants and oppressors. They taxed and made wars entirely for their dynastic benefit. Kings were despots, 'the people' were their helpless victims, poverty-stricken, famished and ground under by the pair of boots that trampled them – the Monarchy (the aristocratic élite) and the Clergy (also land-owners).

The second stage of history (from this viewpoint) was the willed and legislated society. From the moral point of view it declared the emergence of the New Man, virtuous and imposing the good. It was presented as dynamic. Its dominant condition was the smashing of the enslaving monarchic and 'divinely ordained' system, and the creation of the new rule of man in a post-christian, that is, atheist condition.

'The people' ruled – power had passed

to the formerly enslaved masses. The new leaders of society were liberators, dispensing justice and freedom. The first stage of history (the 'Ancien Régime') was ANCIENT. The second stage of history (la Révolution) was MODERN.

This is what the doctrine of evolution conveniently underwrites: that everything happening now is automatically better than what came before, and whatever errors are made on the road of Progress are themselves on their way to being corrected and evolved out of. Democracy, therefore, is claimed to be imperfect, but still the best system ever devised. In the appropriately cynical words of Winston Churchill, it is "the worst form of government – except for all the others that have been tried." This refers of course to Democracy as currently understood, certainly not its early Greek form, which was based on direct representation of the landed and wealthy, with a large slave underclass – although perhaps that is not quite as dissimilar as it seems.

Anything not democratic is automatically Bad, Tyrannical and based on Fear. It is not permitted to publicly contemplate alternatives. This absolutism bears the mark of idolatry and stems from the doctrine of time being something infinite which we progress along, getting better and better.

From this we have the adjective 'progressive', which is now used to mean anything good, simply because it is supposed to be further along the evolutionary conveyor belt than whatever its proponents oppose. The implications of seeing chronological time as absolute are devastating. Whereas, realising that time, although seemingly long, is entirely finite, goes hand in hand with realising what is beyond time. And that is Allah.

Idolatry is unnatural and against the nature of existence and how things are set up. The degree to which you have wrong foundations will be the degree to which you go wrong.

The idol of time is to attribute infiniteness to what is finite, thus saying something untrue on a foundation level. The Message of Islam corrects this, just as other revealed religions did before, but no longer can.

The Messenger of Allah, may Allah bless him and grant him peace, said, "The best of what I or any of the Prophets have said is 'no god, only Allah, alone without partner'," and he encouraged his followers to say 'La ilaha illallah' (no god, only Allah) frequently. They and later Muslims took this on and formalised it in what is known as 'Dhikr' – remembrance. One evening, my Master, may Allah reward him, said to us, "Gather again at the Sunrise Prayer tomorrow and recite 'La ilaha illallah' ten thousand times." We did so, finishing after midday, and afterwards we were changed and we became inseparable and love grew between us. The practice of remembering Allah in His Uniqueness changes the one who does it.

TRANSMISSION

Islam has been transmitted to us by different channels. You need to know this. The Qur'an is memorised by young men and women across the world who sit on the floor, face to face with teachers who themselves have memorised it the same way, in a chain uninterrupted from the time when the Messenger recited it to his Companions, sitting on the ground in Makkah and Madinah. The transmission of Qur'an is not something inherently old. Nor has this process changed and become something new. It is eminently human.

The same happened with knowledge of the Law,

which is called Fiqh, the sayings of the Messenger and his Companions, which are known as Hadith, and social transactions and behaviour, which are 'Amal. They have been transmitted down to us.

Oral transmission and witnessing at first hand have been the main route for all this knowledge – supported by the written word.

What we could call the inner condition and inner actions of the Messenger of Allah, may Allah bless him and grant him peace – without which Islam would not have any reality – were also transmitted to his Companions face-to-face. This goes beyond the realm of words. It goes beyond even his character. It is a matter of the inward, and the inward of the inward.

When you sit with another person, something passes between you besides that which you discuss, see, hear, feel and smell. It is something not spoken or seen. It is not a mystery: it happens all of the time to everyone. A person of darkness will give you some of their darkness. A person of light will give you some of their light.

The Messenger of Allah was light: nothing about him was dark, despite him being subject to all the disparate conditions of humanity (except dishonesty, stupidity and repellent forms of illness and forgetfulness, which Allah protected all the Prophets from). His states were never in contradiction to what came to him from his Lord in every moment. He was in submission to his Lord's all-pervading command not only in the sense of outward rulings, but in the sense of his heart. He had total integrity. He was true.

This condition is man's highest possibility. It exists and will always exist. The Messenger of Allah said, "There will always be forty of my community with the station of Ibrahim." The Prophet Ibrahim (Abraham) is called 'Khalil' in the Qur'an, which means Close Friend, but the word comes from an Arabic root which means to be devoted, as well as to be soaked in something to the point where you are fully permeated.

Such people are imbued with love. Nobody can attain to this station in its fullness except by accompanying one who has it. The exception proves the rule. It is attained by being with and striving to follow the indications of such a person, but at the same time it is a gift from Reality without being given to anybody by anyone or being subject to cause and effect at all. These contradictory statements are not fully reconciled except in the one whose condition this is. We will call this person the Shaykh of Ma'rifa, but it is a spiritual station, not a title.

Muhammad, may Allah bless him and grant him peace, transmitted this station to whomever of his Companions Allah willed, and it was passed from those to others. Some – many – of these rivers flowing out from the Messenger went only so far, then dried up. Nor was it necessarily bequeathed down the bloodline. There is a nobility assured to the genetic descendants of the Messenger, but that was still a matter of genetics, whereas this knowledge is not. Of all the rivers of this knowledge that flowed from the Messenger, there are two main ones that continue to be known to this day. One was from the Messenger to Sayyiduna Abu Bakr and onwards from him, the other was the Messenger to Sayyiduna Ali and onwards from him, may Allah be pleased with them all.

My Master, may Allah have mercy on him and reward him, received this inward knowledge from the latter river, by being in the presence of the gnostic of Allah and scholar, Shaykh Muhammad ibn al-Habib. He in turn got it from Sayyidi Muhammad ibn 'Ali, who took it face to face from Sayyidi al-'Arabi al-Huwari, who received it from Sayyidi Muhammad al-'Arabi, who had it directly by sitting with Sayyidi Ahmad al-Badawi, who was among the many given it by his teacher Moulay al-'Arabi ad-Darqawi, who uniquely took it from the great gnostic Sayyidi 'Ali al-Jamal, who took it from Sayyidi al-'Arabi ibn 'Abdullah, who took it from Sayyidi Ahmad ibn 'Abdullah, from Sayyidi Qasim al-Khassasi, from Sayyidi Muhammad ibn 'Abdullah, from Sayyidi 'Abdur-Rahman al-Fasi, from Sayyidi Yusuf al-Fasi, from Sayyidi 'Abdur-Rahman al-Majdhub, from Sayyidi 'Ali ad-Duwwar, from Sayyidi Ibrahim al-Fahham, from Sayyidi Ahmad Zarruq – and we have reached back to the 15th century by this point. He in turn took it from Sayyidi Ahmad al-Hadrami, from Sayyidi Yahya al-Qadiri, from Sayyidi 'Ali Wafa, from his father Sayyidi Muhammad Wafa, from Sayyidi Dawud al-Bakhili, from Sayyidi Ahmad ibn 'Ata'illah (14th century), from Sayyidi Abu'l-'Abbas al-Mursi, from Sayyidi Abu'l-Hasan ash-Shadhili who took it from Sayyidi 'Abdus-Salam ibn Mashish, and ash-Shadhili also took from Sayyidi Muhammad ibn Harazim, from Sayyidi Muhammad Salih, from Sayyidi Abu Madyan al-Ghawth, from Mawlana 'Abdul-Qadir al-Jilani, from Sayyidi Abu Sa'id al-Mubarak, from Sayyidi Abu'l-Hasan al-Hukkari, from Sayyidi at-Tartusi, from Sayyidi ash-Shibli, from Imam Junayd who lived in Baghdad in the 9th century and took this knowledge from Sayyidi as-Sari as-Saqati, from Sayyidi Ma'ruf al-Karkhi, from Sayyidi Da'ud at-Ta'i, from Sayyidi Habib al-'Ajami, from al-Hasan al-Basri, who took it from the son-in-law of the Messenger, Sayyiduna 'Ali ibn Abi Talib, may Allah be pleased with him and honour his face, who was given it by the Messenger of Allah, may Allah bless him and grant him peace, who was given it by the Angel Jibril, the Trustworthy, who was given it from the One Whose majesty is vast, and Whose Names and Attributes are pure, the Lord of the Worlds.

This is one of the chains by which this inward knowledge has come down to us.

This inward knowledge is not passed from father to son like the inheritance of this world – and the exception proves the rule. This despite the fact that children do naturally take on inward aspects of their parents as well as outward behaviours, genetic aspects and the inheritance of possessions. But the relationship between Shaykh of Ma'rifa and student must go beyond that.

There are two principal signs that such a chain of transmission has gone from something living to something dead. The first is that transmission becomes from father to son only: a genetic chain.

Many chains, or silsilas, have become like this. Their claimants then attribute a spiritual station to the living heir, or simply say their Shaykh is the long-deceased ancestor whose progeny maintain guardianship over his legacy. Neither of these is what is meant here by the Shaykh of Ma'rifa, the one with direct knowledge of Allah. The groupings that exist around such dead chains are like spiritual clubs at best, sustained by and sustaining the baraka of the last true Knower of Allah in the line. At worst they become business enterprises or repositories for the deluded.

The second sign of a dead chain of transmission is that its adherents do not insist on the Deen of Islam.

The Shaykh of Ma'rifa has nothing to do with this, nor does his grouping. His students are called murids, from the word 'irada' – 'to want' or 'to will' – because they want this knowledge. They want nearness to Allah. And they attach themselves to him because he has it and they want it. You could say they are called murid because they have subsumed their own will to his. Without wanting – without longing – this knowledge cannot be acquired. It is not information. It is what grows inside you when the fire of love is kindled.

TRANSFORMATION

If you wish to be on the Path of this inward knowledge, then you must be Muslim. This Shaykh of Ma'rifa will insist on the Shari'a of Islam and be its foremost upholder because he has the closest and most intimate knowledge of Allah and His Messenger. If he denies the need for the Shari'a of Islam, he is a charlatan and has nothing to offer but illusion and destruction. Shaykh Muhammad ibn al-Habib, rahimahullah, my Master's first Shaykh, said, "If a man does not follow the Shari'a of Muhammad, leave him, even if he comes to you flying on a carpet."

The path of inward knowledge of Allah is called Tasawwuf. This has been rendered as 'Sufism' in English but we will retain the Arabic term.

Once you are Muslim, if you wish to travel this Path of inward illumination, you must find a living man who has this knowledge.

You cannot simultaneously have two Shaykhs of this knowledge, because the heart cannot go in two directions. You can have many teachers of the Law, multiple teachers of Qur'an, but only one Shaykh of Ma'rifa who instructs you. If your Shaykh passes away or your connection with him finishes, you may have another.

This kind of man who is able to guide people on the path to knowledge of Allah is also known as the Shaykh of Tariqa, the Tariqa being both the Way itself and the chain to which he belongs. He is also called the Shaykh of Tarbiya or Shaykh of Instruction. He gives his murids general instructions and he gives them particular instructions. And he gives to them by other means.

General instructions include regular recitations, such as the Ratib al-Haddad or the Wird of the Habibiyya-Darqawiyya. These are compilations of supplications, Qur'an and other teachings composed by the Shaykh or his predecessors, whose regular repetition is beneficial to their people. He may also, or instead, order the recitation of particular suras of Qur'an such as Surat al-Waqi'a, which was used as a Wird by Shaykh Ahmad al-'Alawi of Mostaghanem. And there may be other practices which such a Shaykh gives his people to do, such as the Khalwa – retreat – and the recitation of the Name of Allah as practised by the Shadhili Tariqa, alone in the night, drawing out the second consonant, and as taught by my Master, may Allah be pleased with him.

Particular instructions are given to murids according to their needs, strengths, weaknesses, circumstances and inclinations. These might be other dhikrs, such as repeating the Qur'anic phrase 'Hasbunallah wa ni'mal wakil' – Allah is enough for us and the best Guardian – a certain number of times, or more comprehensive actions like going on Hajj, once or more than once, or actions such as feeding people, marrying, keeping company and avoiding certain things such as a particular activity or particular behaviour. He may also instruct someone to move from a place to another place, which, if done for the sake of Islam, is the Sunna of Hijra.

And he instructs by subtle means that cannot be described because they are beyond the reach of words. My Master, may Allah have mercy on him, was like that. To taste this, you will have to find its people.

All of these transactions are part of the Sunna – the life-practice – of Muhammad, may Allah bless him and grant him peace, and his Companions. The Shaykh is the one who knows, by the gift Allah has given him, which aspects of the vast Sunna to emphasise for each person.

He sees what has ensnared the murid and knows the way out. He sees the illusion under which he is labouring and shows him it so that he can abandon it. This can be bitter medicine, or it can be sweet. He becomes present in the murid's heart and his mind's eye. He may or may not appear to him in dreams or visions, but the basis of transmission is not dreams. It is the face-to-face encounter. Miracles may or may not appear from him. This process is not about miracles. Miracles will only appear if they are what are needed for the murid.

The Shaykh of Instruction knows how to bring the hearts of the murids to life. He knows the sicknesses of his people in his age and he knows the cures. He knows when to draw the murid close and give him attention, and when to push him away and ignore him. His words are teaching. His silence is teaching. His actions are teaching. His refraining from action is teaching. This too is all from the Sunna of Muhammad, may Allah bless him and grant him peace.

He helps the murid break the habits that enslave him. He sees when the murid has begun to rely on worship, rather than the One Worshipped. This too is the Sunna of Sayyiduna Muhammad. Aisha, may Allah be pleased with her, said, "The Messenger of Allah, may Allah bless him and grant him peace, would fast until we said, 'He will not break it.' He would not fast until we said, 'He does not fast.'" And Anas said, "When you did not want to see him praying at night, you would only see him praying. When you did not wish to see him sleeping, you only saw him sleeping."

This is what the people of the inward knowledge call 'the breaking of norms'. When something becomes fixed for someone, it is broken so that his life transforms from something solid to something fluid, turning the murid away from ritual for ritual's sake. This is from the Sunna of Sayyiduna Muhammad, may Allah bless him and grant him peace, who brought a living transaction which is still here for us now, anywhere we are, whenever we look to the Lord Who is present and not absent and keep company with His people.

Not only are actions like feeding and hosting people Sunna. So too is the act of him instructing his Companions to do these things and leading by example, which took place in a living context in response to people and events, not as a long list of good behaviours which you have to memorise. It was not in books until later, and its going into books was a descent from its station. It was lived, and they lived it. Again: one of the exchanges most commonly recorded in the vast Hadith literature is when the Messenger would ask his Companions a rhetorical question: "Shall I tell you about such-and-such...?" and they would answer, "Allah and His Messenger know best." Devolving to the one with clear knowledge is part of the knowledge process.

Much of the inward knowledge passes from the Shaykh of Ma'rifa to the murid by what one might call 'osmosis'. And this is magnified by the murids keeping company together so that the knowledge spreads among them. By it, the murid becomes a blessing for others.

How does the Shaykh do all of these things? It is not a 'specially acquired skill'. It is not a 'talent'. It is not something he got through learning or by studying or undergoing some secret ritual.

Rather, Allah says in a Hadith Qudsi – which is a narration directly from Allah, through but not from the Messenger, and not part of the Qur'an:

> My slave does not approach Me by anything more beloved to Me than the things I

have made obligatory on him. He continues to draw near to Me by voluntary actions so that I love him. When I love him, I am his hearing with which he hears, his seeing with which he sees, his hand with which he strikes and his foot with which he walks.

That is the station of the Shaykh of Ma'rifa.

As the murid progresses further along this Path, he aspires to become a refined receptacle and a rarefied spirit, ready for the arrival of knowledge of Allah, which is by Divine gift which cannot be brought forward or be forestalled.

The people who understand that this knowledge exists, believe in it and set out for it are called, in the terminology of Tasawwuf, the Elite. The ones who arrive at it are called the Elite of the Elite. Allah, may He be exalted, after describing the common people of wrong action and the common people of right action, separates them out as the Forerunners (Sabiqun) in His Noble Book,

وَكُنتُمْ أَزْوَٰجًا ثَلَٰثَةً ۝ فَأَصْحَٰبُ ٱلْمَيْمَنَةِ مَآ أَصْحَٰبُ ٱلْمَيْمَنَةِ ۝ وَأَصْحَٰبُ ٱلْمَشْـَٔمَةِ مَآ أَصْحَٰبُ ٱلْمَشْـَٔمَةِ ۝ وَٱلسَّٰبِقُونَ ٱلسَّٰبِقُونَ ۝ أُو۟لَٰٓئِكَ ٱلْمُقَرَّبُونَ ۝ فِى جَنَّٰتِ ٱلنَّعِيمِ ۝ ثُلَّةٌ مِّنَ ٱلْأَوَّلِينَ ۝ وَقَلِيلٌ مِّنَ ٱلْءَاخِرِينَ ۝

And you will be classed into three:
the Companions of the Right:
what of the Companions of the Right?
the Companions of the Left:
what of the Companions of the Left?
and the Forerunners,
the Forerunners.

Those are the Ones Brought Near
in Gardens of Delight.
A large group of the earlier people
but few of the later ones.

THE PATH

The greatest idol is the self. The way of the Muslim is to apostatise from believing in the self. This is the Path of Tasawwuf. Liberation in the world and society is impossible without a commitment to liberation from the self. And vice versa.

My Master, may Allah have mercy on him, wrote:

> Tasawwuf is the science of the journey to the King.

He means the journey to knowledge of Allah. The

great Shaykh of our spiritual lineage, Ahmad ibn 'Ajiba, says in his book, 'The Basic Research':

> As-Sahilli has given us an example which concerns the travel of meaning that takes one to the Presence –

meaning the Presence of Allah.

> He said, "The Presence is like a great King who appeared in the east. He sent messengers to introduce Himself to people and make them yearn for His presence because of His generosity and His excellent attributes. There are those who refuse to obey Him, and they are the kafirun.

The Companions of the Left.

> There are those who obey, but are unable to go to Him, either because they are heavily burdened or because they do not love the King enough. These are the common Muslims who trust in the Unseen.

The Companions of the Right.

There are those who yearn for travel and they exchange their blood and spirit to arrive at Him,

The Forerunners.

– and then the messengers, or whoever represents them, say to this third type of man, 'Here we are, travelling with you and showing you the path.' The King has built houses along the path for His guests, and He has equipped them with water and gardens and flowers, and each successive house is better than the last. So if the messengers or their representatives take the people to these houses, some of them want to dwell in them. Then the messengers say to these, 'The goal is further ahead.' So they continue to travel with them from one place to another and from Station to Station until they arrive at the King. When they see the King with acceptance and generosity, that is their Station and their dwelling place."

My Master continues:

The preferred etymology of Tasawwuf is that

it derives from suf, wool. Shaykh Hasan al-Basri said, "I saw forty of the people of Badr and they all wore wool."

The people of Badr were those who fought with the Messenger in the famous Battle of Badr and therefore some of the closest Companions. It is also said that the word Tasawwuf derives from the Ahl as-Suffa, the people of the Veranda, which was where some of the poorest Companions most dedicated to worship spent their time – outside the house of the Prophet, may Allah bless him and grant him peace.

And it is also said that it derives from the word 'safaa', meaning purity and clarity.

> This means that the Sufi – tasawwafa – has put on the wool.

Imam Malik said about Tasawwuf:

مَن تَفَقَّهَ وَلَمْ يَتَصَوَّفْ فَقَدْ تَفَسَّقَ

وَمَن تَصَوَّفَ وَلَمْ يَتَفَقَّهْ فَقَدْ تَزَندَقَ

وَمَن جَمَعَ بَيْنَهُمَا فَقَدْ تَحَقَّقَ

"Whoever practices Fiqh but does not practice Tasawwuf will be corrupted, and whoever practices Tasawwuf but does not practice Fiqh – i.e. does not obey the Law – will be a heretic. Whoever combines them both will realise the Truth."

> This is distinct from those who confirm the way of Islam with the tongue and by book learning. It is taking the ancient way, the primordial path of direct experience of the Real.

This primordial path is not what perennialists say: that the Path does not require the Shari'a, or that ultimately all religions are the same. Such statements are an attack on Islam and they negate the Messenger of Allah, may Allah bless him and grant him peace.

> Junayd said: "The Sufi is like the earth, filth is flung on it but roses grow from it."

Ignorant people attack the people of this Path. Ahmad Ibn 'Ajiba says: "The more filth is thrown, the more bounty there is."

> He also said, "The Sufi is like the earth which supports the innocent and the guilty, like the

sky which shades everything, like the rain which washes everything."

One of the men of knowledge, in his early days, left his wallet lying in the teaching lodge of my Master's Shaykh, Shaykh Muhammad ibn al-Habib. The Shaykh became angry at him, saying that he would turn his fuqara into thieves by putting temptation in front of them. Theft is punishable in the Law, which the Sufi is the first to uphold. But he saw the guilt of the innocent and the innocence of the guilty. It is like Junayd said: "The Sufi supports the innocent and the guilty." One of the Shaykhs said, "We are like the streets: everyone passes through us, the good and the bad, the obedient and the disobedient."

> The Sufi is universal. He has reduced and then eliminated the marks of selfhood to allow a clear view of the cosmic reality.

'Cosmic' here does not mean interstellar: it means the sum of all created things. The Sufi understands the way the entire universe works, because the workings of his self no longer veil it from him. Shaykh Muhammad ibn al-Habib says in his collection of teaching-poems, known as the Diwan:

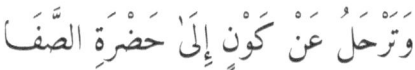

You will journey from the cosmos
to the presence of Purity.

My Master continues:

> He has rolled up the cosmos in its turn and obliterated it. He has gone beyond.

He has gone beyond knowledge of the created universe, because that was not his objective.

> The Sufi has said "Allah" – until he has understood.

Allah says in Qur'an, Al-An'am 92:

Say: "Allah!"

We are ordered to say "Allah". The person of this Path has followed this order until he has understood. When I first spent time with the people of this Path, I noticed that they said "Allah" at every opportunity. Even when something took them by surprise: "Allah!" It was their exclamation for everything and their explanation for everything. My Master continues:

> All men and women play in the world like children.

Qur'an, Al-An'am 92:

$$ثُمَّ ذَرْهُمْ فِي خَوْضِهِمْ يَلْعَبُونَ$$

Then leave them engrossed in playing their games.

The order in Qur'an to say "Allah" is followed by the instruction to leave others engrossed in their games, which is, on one level, acting in the world as if it were all there is.

> The Sufi's task is to recognise the end in the beginning, accept the beginning in the end

It is said that the person of this Path weeps at the news of a birth – the hardness of life lies ahead – and rejoices at the funeral – the job is done, he died Muslim having lived a good life. He will be rewarded.

– arrive at the unified view. When the outward opposites are the same –

This means good and bad, light and dark, cold and hot, constriction and expansion, ease and difficulty are all seen as coming from the Lord. Suffering and joy are still there, but they are transformed.

– and the instant is presence, and the heart is serene, empty and full –

empty of the self and full of the light of Allah.
Quran, Surat an-Nur 35:

Light on light.

– the one in the woollen cloak has been robed with the robe of honour and is complete.

My Master continues:

The Imam

he means Imam Junayd of Baghdad

also said: "If I had known of any science greater than Tasawwuf I would have gone to it, even on my hands and knees."

Ibn 'Ajiba says that Tasawwuf is the greatest knowledge, since knowledge is ranked according to its subject, and Tasawwuf is the science of knowledge of Allah.

My Master continues:

"There is no road to the realities except on the tongue of the Shari'a," said Shaykh al-Akbar.

Shaykh al-Akbar means the Greatest Shaykh and it refers to Muhyiddin ibn 'Arabi.

The Shari'a of Islam is the confirmation that there is no divinity but Allah and that Muhammad is the Messenger of Allah. It is to pray five times daily the ritual prostrations. It is to fast the month of Ramadan. It is to pay the Zakat tax of wealth. It is to take, if possible, the Hajj to the pure House of Allah and the plain of 'Arafat.

It is based on these and confirms that the one following the Shari'a has elected to live within the broad moral parameters set down in the Qur'anic commands and according to the guidance within the Sunna, the life-pattern of Muhammad, blessings of Allah and peace be upon him. Having accepted the Shari'a is the deep cognition that the human creature is limited, is in a body, and thus, like all bodies in the physical world, obeys given laws. There is no compulsion in the life-transaction –

Qur'an, Surat al-Baqara 255:

$$\text{لَآ إِكْرَاهَ فِى ٱلدِّينِ}$$

There is no compulsion in the Deen.

'The Deen' means the life-transaction, another way of describing Islam.

> – thus it cannot be called 'organised religion' – no – it is the self-chosen pattern of life one has adopted in order to deepen knowledge until one reaches one's own source, one's spring of life, to drink of the water of illumination.
> Shari'a thus implies recognition of biological laws that function at every level of existence. Thus, we observe that the kafirun,

those who reject, nevertheless follow their Shari'a.

Allah says in Qur'an, commanding the Muslims to address the kafirun:

> You have your deen
> and I have my deen

Every person sets up a Shari'a, improvised yet functional.

Every person lives by the rules they choose to live by, whether consciously or not, whether legitimate or not, whether Divinely ordained or not. Those who experience unseen realities (or imagine they do) but do not have Prophetic teaching to identify them, concoct their own explanations for them, with no Prophetic legitimacy.

> Our Shari'a is all mercy, while theirs is always revealed to be cruel, repressive and narrow. Ours is from the Best of Creation, beloved by millions of human beings.

The Messenger Muhammad, may Allah bless him and grant him peace, beloved by billions.

Theirs is a dark shadow from lone imaginings.

My Master continues:

> The Path lies between the two opposites, Shari'a and Haqiqa. It is identifiable by its outward, and confirmed by its inward. Just as Shari'a can also be called Islam, so Tariqat may be called Iman – acceptance. Iman is acceptance. Iman is acceptance of Allah, His Books, His Messengers, His Angels, the Last Day, the Balance, the Decree.

This is from the definition of Iman given in perhaps the most famous Hadith of all, known as the Hadith of Jibril. Ahmad ibn 'Ajiba, may Allah be pleased with him, says, "The Tariqa is a result of the Shari'a. The Shari'a is for the correction of the outward limbs, and that leads to the Tariqa, which is the correction of the inward secret. This, in its turn, leads to the Haqiqa, which is the removal of the veil and the witnessing of the Beloved beyond the veil. Let us say that Shari'a is to worship Him, Tariqa is to travel to Him and Haqiqa is to witness Him."

> It is the interiorisation of the cosmic landscape, from creational realities in event –

He is referring to the things which happen in the created world, and the interiorisation of the understanding that they happen by the Decree of Allah,

> – to a personal cosmic landscape in vision. All these explain and interpret the meanings of the dual nature of existence and its unitary secret.

By this interiorisation the traveller gains an understanding of his life and the way existence works.

> Tariqat is coming out from the safe place of ordinary existence into the alien existence of search.

It is a journey. Or you could say, it is awakening, where before you were asleep.

> It means abandoning the private project as a meaning to life, that is, the family.

He means abandoning the idea that your family is the highest meaning to your life. He does not mean abandoning the family, although for some, it has meant that.

Allah, glory be to Him, has warned that that is a trap for you.

Qur'an, At-Taghabun 14-15:

$$\text{يَٰٓأَيُّهَا ٱلَّذِينَ ءَامَنُوٓا۟ إِنَّ مِنْ أَزْوَٰجِكُمْ وَأَوْلَٰدِكُمْ عَدُوًّا لَّكُمْ فَٱحْذَرُوهُمْ ۚ وَإِن تَعْفُوا۟ وَتَصْفَحُوا۟ وَتَغْفِرُوا۟ فَإِنَّ ٱللَّهَ غَفُورٌ رَّحِيمٌ ۝ إِنَّمَآ أَمْوَٰلُكُمْ وَأَوْلَٰدُكُمْ فِتْنَةٌ ۚ وَٱللَّهُ عِندَهُۥٓ أَجْرٌ عَظِيمٌ ۝}$$

You who have Iman!
some of your wives and children
are an enemy to you,
so be wary of them.
But if you pardon and exonerate and forgive,
Allah is Ever-Forgiving, Most Merciful.
Your wealth and children are a trial.
But with Allah there is an immense reward.

It means abandoning the public project which is the society and its promise of future rewards for slavery to it.

He does not mean leaving society and going to live alone in the wilderness or in the countryside to set up a community cut off from everyone else. He means abandoning society as a means to future, material rewards and as a meaning to life.

> The future reward of the seeker is now in the Unseen and after death, not at the end of life. It means abandoning the autobiographical project of fame and fulfilment, for the self has become for the seeker, an enemy.
> The self is an enemy –

The Sufic strategy against the self-as-enemy is not to punish it for every single thing it seeks, but rather to rein it in and discipline it with wisdom. Sometimes this can even mean giving it what it wants, since punitive self-denial is one of the stratagems of the self. If a person was brought up being denied everything, then their self will seek to perpetuate the pattern as its way of affirming its existence and will hijack the Sufic instruction of doing-without and continue to inflict parental deprivation on itself. The Shaykh and the murids are the guide in discerning this, until you have developed your own discrimination. Unless, that is, the historical damage is so severe that somebody is not equipped for the Path. Then they cannot embark unless they heal the wound. The Path is not for the mentally ill and is dangerous for them.

My Master continues regarding the self:

> that is, until it is transformed into its luminous reality which is pure spirit.

Because, once the self is reined in, it transforms, which means to die as self and come forth as Ruh, or spirit. Ruh and self – called 'nafs' in the terminology of the Path and in Qur'an – are two descriptions of the same thing, looked at from opposite aspects.

> Shari'a is submitting. Tariqat is handing over.
> Haqiqa is victory.

My Master continues:

> Haqiqaat, the realities, are the inward illuminations of knowledge which flood the heart of the seeker. It is the realm of meanings, as Shari'a is the realm of the senses. As one is the science of the outward, the other is the science of the inward. There is no way to its experience but by submission to the

fact of being human, being mortal, an in-time creature.

In other words, we cannot behave as if nothing matters, even though, from the point of view of the Haqiqa, nothing does. If we are speaking of Haqiqa, then things and events do not matter, since they are all and only by the Decree of our Lord. But the door to the Haqiqa and the realm of meanings is through its opposite, the Shari'a and the realm of senses: the world of created things and actions, in which things do matter. If we are speaking of Shari'a, it is all about what matters. Being an in-time creature means obeying wisdom, which is Shari'a. This is the true affirmation of Unity, because it acknowledges that Allah has set up our existence as bodies, choices, actions and volition. To deny the need to be Muslim is to limit Allah in His generosity. He has provided a way to correct the outward and so correct the inward.

Once Shari'a is submitted to, then the seeker on the Path realises that he has come from non-existence and is going to non-existence.

Qur'an, Baqara 155:

The Path

> We belong to Allah
> and to Him we will return.

Qur'an, 'Abasa 18-21:

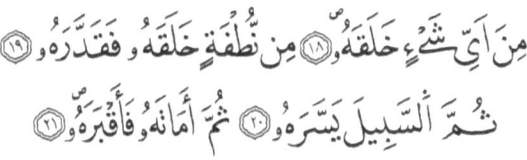

> From what thing did He create him?
> From a drop of sperm He created him
> and proportioned him.
> Then He eases the way for him.
> Then He causes him to die and buries him.

My Master continues:

> The time is short. It must be seized. Cut through! In this world everything is spectacle, yet everywhere the people are blind. They cannot bear to see that the world's rewards do not bring satisfaction to its people. This is not meant to be the zone of visions — that is the next world, after death. This is the zone of action. To reach the status of the whole human being is not possible without a breaking of norms. Breaking of norms is the Path.

Enter Islam

Breaking norms, as we have seen, is going against the self, because the self is composed of habits and norms. Shaykh Moulay al-'Arabi ad-Darqawi, one of the Masters of our Tariqa, tells in his 'Letters' of a Christian who would touch the disease of other Christians with his hand, and they would be healed. News of him spread through the lands until it reached one of the Friends of Allah. He said to himself, "This is one of the miracles of the Friends of Allah which no-one who is a kafir and rejects Allah the Exalted can perform. This is impossible. It is unheard-of! By Allah, I will go and visit him and ask him about what he does." He got there and the Christian said to him, "I only do what is heavy for my self and I never do what is light for it." He replied, "If you are sincere in your claim, then show your self Islam and see whether it is heavy or light for it." He showed it Islam and it was heavier for it than anything before had been. He confirmed and admitted that to the Friend of Allah, may Allah be pleased with him, who said to the Christian: "Then become Muslim if you are sincere in what you say." He could do nothing except become Muslim immediately at his hand.

> Its fruits are witnessing and illumination. Yet these belong to after-death in the sensory.

Thus to reach vision in the meaning-realm means to die the death of meaning before the sensory death. "Die before you die," says the famous Hadith.

It is re-iterated in many others from the Sahih

The Sahih refers to the main collections of Hadith –

such as the instruction "Make yourselves as the inhabitants of the grave."

This is an instruction – in other words, it is formulated as an order and we have to do it.

This does not suggest giving up life but that to know the great knowledge there must be practice – and that is its instruction.

If you desire Haqiqa – reconcile yourself – your life can never be the same again. "Man is asleep. When he dies he wakes up!" Haqiqa is waking up. Ihsan.

In other words, where Shari'a is called Islam and Tariqa is called Iman, Haqiqa is called Ihsan, which is, in the well-known words of the Messenger: "To worship Allah as if you see Him, and while you do not see Him, know that He sees you."

RIBA

To set out on the path of knowledge you must be committed to Allah's commands and prohinitions, and thus engage in society. Were Islam an established reality, that might not be the case. But it is not. Putting right the inward means putting right the outward. And in this age we live in, this entails an unavoidable confrontation with riba. Riba is the sickness of the age.

The great Imam Malik, who lived in the second century of Islam, counselled that in a time of licentiousness, lean heavily on the laws prohibiting adultery and fornication; in a time of widespread alcoholism, lean heavily on the laws prohibiting drinking. Neither of these is the foremost affliction among Muslims at this time, despite whatever activities may go on. What is widespread among them – and among all of mankind – is riba.

Allah says in His Noble Book:

$$وَأَحَلَّ ٱللَّهُ ٱلْبَيْعَ وَحَرَّمَ ٱلرِّبَوٰاْ$$

Allah has permitted trade and forbidden riba.

And Allah says,

$$ٱلَّذِينَ يَأْكُلُونَ ٱلرِّبَوٰاْ لَا يَقُومُونَ إِلَّا كَمَا يَقُومُ ٱلَّذِي يَتَخَبَّطُهُ ٱلشَّيْطَانُ مِنَ ٱلْمَسِّ$$

> Those who practise riba
> will not rise from the grave
> except as someone driven mad
> by Shaytan's touch.

The Messenger of Allah, may Allah bless him and grant him peace, counselled his community to avoid riba, even to a blade of grass. He said, "A dirham of riba which a man consumes knowingly is worse with Allah than fornicating thirty-six times," and, "There are seventy-two kinds of riba, the least of which is like a man committing incest with his mother."

So what is this thing called riba which is so strongly forbidden and which is the root cause of much of the bad we see around us today? What is this riba which drives people and whole societies mad? What is this riba which only the Muslims can fully identify and whose unique cure lies in obedience to Allah through the Deen of Islam?

Imam Malik, may Allah be pleased with him, was one of the greatest early jurists of Islam. While active as the undisputed legal authority of his time, handing down judgments and receiving delegations from across the Muslim world seeking knowledge, he also composed the first written formulation of Islam, called the 'Muwatta'. This does not mean he made up anything new. It means that before that, in Madinah – which was the city established by the Prophet as the living, transacting society of Islam – the natural life transaction which is Islam was known and practiced without it needing to be recorded in written form.

Malik was born 81 years after the death of the Prophet, may Allah bless him and grant him peace, and became the undisputed authority in Madinah on the way things were done there in the time of the Prophet and in the two generations afterwards, during which the Deen was still whole and unbroken. Over half of his book is about social and business transactions, as distinct from acts of worship.

To understand riba, let us look at some of the many things he says about it as understood by those early generations.

EARLY NARRATIONS CONCERNING RIBA

In his Muwatta it says:

> Yahya related to me from Malik that he had heard that receipts were given to people in the time of Marwan ibn al-Hakam (– about 60 years after Islam appeared in Madinah –) for the produce of the market at al-Jar. People bought and sold the receipts among themselves before they had taken actual delivery of the goods. Zayd ibn Thabit and one of the other Companions of the Messenger of Allah, may Allah bless him and grant him peace, went to Marwan and said, "Marwan, are you making riba permissible?" He said, "I seek refuge in Allah! What do you mean?" He replied, "These

receipts which people buy and sell before they take delivery of the goods." So Marwan sent guards to round them up and take the receipts from people and return them to their owners.

From this and numerous other accounts we know that riba is more than just 'interest', which Muslims are well known to oppose. It can be an unfair or uncertain delay between a sale and delivery, or between delivery and payment, as well as any unjust increase in a financial transaction. And it can be inherent uncertainty in transactions, as with these receipts. They were uncertain, because the recipient could not know for sure whether they would really be exchangeable for what they were issued for. What, for example, if the issuer died, or no longer had the goods?

Pay close attention, because the wellbeing of all future societies depends on it:

> People bought and sold the receipts among themselves before they had taken actual delivery of the goods.

These receipts were in essence identical to the paper money which, centuries later, began to seep into societies in place of specie currency. Specie currency is gold and silver coinage and has value in its own right, so it is certain. Zayd Ibn Thabit, because he was steeped in the Prophetic practice and the Prophetic clarity, was able to see the evil in these receipts when used as currency, and Marwan ibn al-Hakam possessed the wisdom and authority to put a stop to it.

Sometimes riba can be disguised as convenience. Pay careful attention to this account. 'Ubayd Abu Salih said:

> I sold some drapery to the people of Dar Nakhla on credit. Then I wanted to go to Kufa, so they suggested that I reduce the price for them and they would pay me immediately. I asked Zayd ibn Thabit about it and he said, "I order you not to accept increase or to allow it to anybody."

He forbade this because by offering to pay less, the people of Dar Nakhla were suggesting that 'Ubayd should 'purchase' the bringing-forward of payment, by foregoing a fraction of what had been agreed as the value of the goods. This is of the same nature as interest, because it gives value to the passing of time over money. Allowing such an evaluation gives an immediate and unnatural advantage to people who have money over those who do not, simply by virtue of having it. The outcome is very clear in our times.

All of banking and modern finance are based on this and similar forms of forbidden transaction.

> Malik said, "The Messenger of Allah, may Allah bless him and grant him peace, forbade selling food before getting delivery of it."
>
> Malik said, "The generally agreed-on way of doing things among us in which there is no dispute about buying food – wheat, barley, durra, pearl millet, or any pulse or anything resembling pulses on which zakat is obliged, or condiments of any sort – oil, ghee, honey, vinegar, cheese, sesame oil, milk and so on, is that the buyer should not re-sell any of it until he has taken possession and complete delivery of it."

Again, we see the prohibition of uncertain transactions, since food is such that its exact nature cannot be ascertained until it is there in front of you. This prohibition removes the unnatural speculative element which leads to the twisted aberrations we see today such as 'futures on wheat' (a form of gambling) and the consequences of allowing them. If it appears 'inconvenient', that is only because it is inconvenient to the massive monopolistic megastructures which control our food supply and demand the denaturing of food and land and the crushing of farmers to achieve Growth. They have put out the theory of food shortage, with them as the rescuers, somehow implying that these monopolistic, industrial methods of food production are essential to the survival of mankind. All of that is deception, but it cannot be curbed by trying to limit monopolies or providing alternative, small-scale, organic farms or by people (usually the affluent) buying local. Until the underlying transactions which allow such malformations as we now see in food supply and other industries are forbidden, things will not change. Riba is like cancer. If underlying conditions are conducive, its tumorous growths will evade control and spread to all the organs.

> Malik said, "One should not buy a debt owed by a man whether present or absent, without the confirmation of the one who owes the debt, nor should one buy a debt owed to a man by a dead person even if one knows

what the deceased man has left. This is because to buy it is an uncertain transaction and one does not know whether the transaction will be completed or not."

He said, "The explanation of what is disapproved of in buying a debt owed by someone absent or dead is that it is not known which unknown debtors may have claims on the dead person. If the dead person is liable for another debt, the value which the buyer gives on the strength of the debt may become worthless." Malik said, "There is another fault in it as well. He is buying something which is not guaranteed for him, so if the deal is not completed, what he has paid becomes worthless. This is an uncertain transaction and it is not good."

Malik said, "The disapproved way of doing things about which there is no dispute among us (i.e. in the city left behind by the Prophet and his Companions) is that a man gives a loan to a man for a term, and then the demander reduces it and the one from whom it is demanded pays it in advance. To us that is like someone who delays repaying his debt after it is due to his creditor and his creditor increases his debt." Malik said, "This is nothing but riba – no doubt about it."

Yahya related to me from Malik from 'Uthman ibn Hafs ibn Khalda from Ibn Shihab from Salim ibn 'Abdullah that 'Abdullah ibn 'Umar was asked about a man who took a loan from another man for a set term. The creditor reduced the debt and the man paid it immediately. 'Abdullah ibn 'Umar disliked that and forbade it.

These are just a few excerpts from an enormous corpus of judgments from the first Community of Muslims which apply to trade and financial transactions.

RIBA TODAY

This precise, discerning and clean atmosphere in the Madinah of the Companions and the generations that immediately followed them could hardly contrast more with our situation today. Not only are transactions full of uncertainty and riba. The very currency in which we conduct them is uncertain and decreases over time, because it is being issued out of nothing. Like the receipts of al-Jar, it is tokens of no intrinsic value. It is only money because, like the people at the market of Al-Jar before they were stopped, we agree to use it.

All of us, Muslim or not, have grown up in societies where money is debased into something our ancestors, Muslim or not, would condemn. Inflation and the pumping of money into the financial system by banks and governments are overt riba, because to manufacture tokens out of nothing and then spend them is an unjust transaction and creates uncertainty and an effective theft (= inflation) in every transaction done using the money that already exists. Making this lawful places something that resembles magic into the hands of the licensed practitioners of the technique, allowing them to create wealth ex nihilo. They create token wealth, yet they create no real wealth. They transfer real wealth from everyone else to themselves. It is done by means of an illusion, but the consequences are very real. As they create their wealth, they impoverish, by the devaluation of the pseudo-money-tokens, everyone not entitled to control this process – i.e. the vast majority of mankind. And everyone is subject to the process. Because everyone accepts the tokens, they are seen to have value – but at a terrible cost.

This is a technique of slow bleeding. So how was it that people in the seventh century were able to spot it and stop it, and we are not? Because they referred everything back to Allah and His Messenger, may Allah bless him and grant him peace. Today, alas, even the Muslims have stopped doing that in the realm of the financial. They have fallen for the illusion of riba. Most of the relatively tiny number of Muslim scholars (and a few thinkers from outside the realm of Islam) who have realised this have been a) too weak or frightened to raise their voices, b) in the pay of people who are invested in the system, or c) disregarded when they have raised their voices, so they have not been able to persuade anyone else, let alone their leaders, to desist in the way that Zayd ibn Thabit persuaded Marwan to desist. And the leaders, if they have heard it, have not had the strength or courage or conviction to do anything in the way that Marwan did something.

Meanwhile, money has changed from being worth something in itself – gold or silver, which we know are sound because they were used by the Messenger of Allah and his Companions – firstly into paper tokens called banknotes, and then into mere numbers in bank balances and 'positions' in 'portfolios' and all the euphemistic language that has grown up around these criminal practices. That transformation has allowed 'money' to be created out of nothing. Continuously. And to decrease everyone else's 'money' in its buying power.

This has produced a world in which everything appears to get gradually more expensive. Our financial experience, from birth onwards, is that 'things go up'. It is an illusion, since the real value of the things we buy remains the same, provided the things remain the same. But the numerical effect of inflation creates such a powerful illusion that we are conditioned to think of things getting more expensive. We live in a world of seeming increase in price, and the corollary of that is seeming decrease in what is available to us, down to our very sustenance. Living itself seems to get more difficult.

Economics has become about, and obsessed with, the idol of Growth. If there is no Growth in an economy, it is almost as if national disaster has struck. There is an unexamined compulsion to make everything 'grow'. Humans, in other words, experience everything as shrinking, due to the criminal creation of money out of nothing and the flow of money into ever fewer hands. The vast majority know that something is wrong because so few people have such absolute say on the movement and sale of commodities. It is therefore easy to persuade them that everything must be made to grow and expand just so they can breathe. It is madness to counteract the madness. Countries, cities and businesses are considered worthless junk if they are not growing.

This can be seen as the root cause of man's destruction of our planet, since he has to eat up and consume things without reason, driven by a pathological urge to counter his shrinking 'money' without even understanding what drives him. As long as we seek a technical solution to ecological disaster and fail to see its origins in the criminal financial technique of riba, we will not stop it.

That is a psychological explanation. But it doesn't stop there. Riba breaches the walls of the city of safety, because it introduces another powerful malefic factor. It creates the conditions of war.

RIBA AND UNJUST WAR

War is mankind's most expensive activity. Social welfare, infrastructure, education, health – nothing comes close. When a people go to war, amounts of money are suddenly spent that are not needed at other times. Prior to the arrival of riba in this author's country of origin, England, the natural brake on the nation's warring impulse was the limit to the money that could be raised from its people. A natural tension existed between king and nobles – between whomever wished to pursue war and whomever had the means to finance it. The latter had to be convinced by the former of the need to go to war and the benefits of doing so. If these benefits were seen to exist, the money could be raised. But the money had to be there in the first place. This meant that wars were fought that would benefit those with the means to finance them, but they were also the ones who stood to lose out if the war was lost. And because the nobles were existentially connected to the people they were placed over and on whom their continuance depended, they would consider their needs too, despite the modern propaganda which tells us they didn't.

Not so with the practitioners of riba. With the acceptance of the riba principle and the admission into the social fabric of moneylending as a practice, a third party appeared on the scene who would benefit in both victory and defeat. They did not need persuading as to whether war was beneficial, provided they could see the prospect of returns on the loan. And if there was destruction, they could finance the rebuild.

This is what we see in the emergence of the great financial houses. It is not a criticism of any particular race, although certain groups have been predominant in the activity. To make it a racial matter is to miss the central point. Riba, its principle and practice, is forbidden by Allah, the Creator of the universe. It is unnatural. Wars based on it will inevitably be like those we see today, in which the richest nations in the world and their followers invade and destroy countries for strategic and commercial gain, beneath a rhetoric designed for the home crowd. Rather than bringing a superior social system to the places they conquer, they make them worse. And their fighters, rather than being ennobled by the profound experience of warfare, are broken and deranged by it, then left to decay.

War financed by riba is, on the scale of evil, high. But the coupling of riba with the technological project is yet another tragic outcome of allowing this perverse practice. Banking unleashes technological progress and growth, but on untenable terms. It is the same on a personal level as it is on the social. Prior to the acceptance of riba, someone who wanted something would – unless they entered into a permissible trade transaction in which they also shared the risk – have to a) possess the wealth, b) save up, investing work and time, or c) borrow from someone who would not benefit materially from the lending process. This means that the purchase had to be important enough and that due consideration was necessarily given to whether it really was, because the buyer would have time to reflect on it as he saved, or would have to balance the expenditure against the loss of savings, or would have to persuade the lender, who did not stand to benefit materially. These attenuating factors do not mean things cannot be bought, but they do put the horse back before the cart and they do mean there is a reasonable chance of balance and prudence.

Introduce the loan at interest, and that prudence, that moderating factor, that equilibrium, is swept away. Everything is suddenly available. Furthermore, it is in the interest of the lenders that everything should be made available, and that new things are constantly being invented and produced, coupled with credit, to keep stimulating that aspect of man that finds it hard to resist the new, and to keep feeding the insatiable greed of the lenders, getting money for nothing.

Thus new technical devices are linked for the vast majority of people to credit, as are new cars and new houses. Even clothing. Further up the immense ladder of riba, vast infrastructural projects become the offspring of the extraordinary coupling of technology and banking, to which the highest-achieving minds are encouraged to dedicate their lives.

ABANDONING RIBA

Islam forbids every kind of uncertain, imbalanced and deceitful economic transaction, including interest, the debasement of currency and the creation of currency out of nothing. The punishments for corrupting currency are frightening, and rightly so, because debasing currency ultimately brings forth a delusional society of people bent on a growth which is unnatural and cannot be sustained – bent on destroying the world and each other, all for a growth which is but an illusion.

For the small man on the street, the shrinking nature of his money, and the feeling of slowly drowning, and the fact that his life has become a solely financial project, all have a more immediate effect. It is slowly driving him mad.

Allah says,

$$\text{الَّذِينَ يَأْكُلُونَ الرِّبَوٰا۟ لَا يَقُومُونَ إِلَّا كَمَا يَقُومُ الَّذِي يَتَخَبَّطُهُ الشَّيْطَانُ مِنَ الْمَسِّ}$$

> Those who practise riba
> will not rise from the grave
> except as someone driven mad
> by Shaytan's touch.

The media discourse around Islam is the wrong one. The Deen has come to Western countries not primarily to stop people going for a drink or to make women cover their hair. And certainly not to suggest to lonely and unstable people via the Internet to blow themselves up along with some innocents. Yes, Muslims don't drink and they do dress modestly – men and women – which is a blessing and ennobles them. But those are everyday life things, not foundational ones.

What the Muslims actually have is transmitted openly, face to face, among people who want to please their Creator, and it brings life and hope and health, understanding and meaning. It allows people to understand why it is right to behave with courtesy, generosity and justice. And it allows people to understand the financial crimes perpetrated upon them and the financial pressure they experience. And it gives them – and you if you so wish – something to do about it.

If you want to do something about it, you face a task much more important than secondary moral issues – much more essential to the lives of everyone, and much more exciting and sublime. You have to be Muslim, because only if you submit to Allah can you overpass a way of looking at this that gives a systems answer to what is widely seen as a systems question. Only Muslims really know that wrong money and wrong transactions and wrong economics are contrary to the Divinely created pattern, and only they know the shape of what is right. More importantly, only they are oriented not to 'solving the problem' of riba. They look instead to obeying what Allah has commanded and prohibiting what He has forbidden, in the knowledge that it is Allah Who brought us about and it is Allah Who can bring about what is right, through the actions of those who believe in Him. There is nothing remotely mythical or magical about this. But it does involve belief.

Islam means real currency of inherent value and the equitable contracts of its Law. It means being straight. This never goes out of date. If anything it is the future, because we are languishing in a time of financial decay which will not go on for ever, and upon which future people (if there are any left) will look back with horror and disgust, wondering how such a dark age and such an unnatural and morally twisted society could ever have existed and how humans survived it.

If you want to do something about it you have to be Muslim, because while the remedy does lie in the prohibition of certain kinds of transaction, that prohibition has to be done in obedience to the

Creator. It is not 'the Islamic solution' like some kind of 'heavenly machine'. To think that Islam is the right system as opposed to the wrong system only makes an idol out of Islam.

Actions are required that originate in hearts that want to please their Lord and fear going wrong with their Lord. That is what true worship is. Marwan ibn al-Hakam did not round up the receipts of the market at Al-Jar because he had overlooked a systemic error and wanted to 'fix the system'. He did so because he recognised the superior knowledge of Zayd ibn Thabit as one of the closest Companions of the Messenger of Allah, and did not want to go against what he knew the Prophet, may Allah bless him and grant him peace, had forbidden. Because that would be disobeying Allah.

Allah says in Surat An-Nisa' 79:

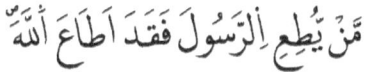

> Whoever obeys the Messenger
> has obeyed Allah.

This is the Message of Islam. The worst thing about terrorism committed 'in the name of Islam' is not the terrible suffering it causes to innocent people.

Enter Islam

The causes of terrorism lie not in Islam. They lie in a departure from Islam, just as they lay in the departure from Christianity in other contexts such as those so well described by Dostoevsky and other deconstructors of nihilism. The worst thing about terrorism is that it prevents people from knowing that the Muslims have a far more urgent message upon which the destiny of mankind pivots. Muslims say what Allah says:

ٱلَّذِينَ يَأْكُلُونَ ٱلرِّبَوٰاْ لَا يَقُومُونَ إِلَّا كَمَا يَقُومُ ٱلَّذِى يَتَخَبَّطُهُ ٱلشَّيْطَٰنُ مِنَ ٱلْمَسِّ ذَٰلِكَ بِأَنَّهُمْ قَالُوٓاْ إِنَّمَا ٱلْبَيْعُ مِثْلُ ٱلرِّبَوٰاْ وَأَحَلَّ ٱللَّهُ ٱلْبَيْعَ وَحَرَّمَ ٱلرِّبَوٰاْ

> Those who practise riba
> will not rise from the grave
> except as someone driven mad
> by Shaytan's touch.
> That is because they say,
> "Trade is the same as riba."
> But Allah has permitted trade
> and He has forbidden riba.

CHRISTIANITY

Muslims do not worship the same God as Christians. Allah does not have a son, neither in reality nor metaphorically. Nothing can be associated with Him. Nothing should be said to be divine alongside Him. It is untrue to say that anything or anyone shares any of His attributes in any way.

Jesus, peace be upon him, was the son of Mary and one of the greatest Prophets, and Muslims esteem him and love him. He was sent to call the Jews back to the teachings of Moses, which were Allah's teachings. Muslims call him 'Isa son of

Maryam. He and his blessed mother are mentioned many times in the highest terms in the Qur'an. The Lady Maryam has a whole chapter named after her, describing her extraordinary story in which there is rich teaching for all time. Qur'an is Revelation. It is true.

Whatever excuses Christians may try to make for why they divide God up into three, and whatever they may mean by that, it is untrue. It is refuted by Allah in the Qur'an.

The first Surah, or chapter, which Muslims are likely to learn as children or when they enter the Deen as adults, after the Fatihah, or Opening, is called Ikhlas, or Sincerity:

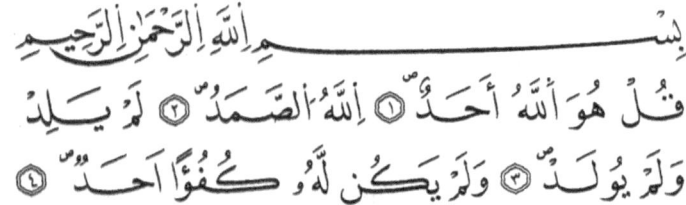

In the name of Allah, All-Merciful, Most Merciful
Say: "He is Allah, Absolute Oneness,
Allah, the Everlasting Sustainer of all.
He has not given birth and was not born.
And no one is comparable to Him."

Such is the importance of this short Surah that

Christianity

the Messenger of Allah, may Allah bless him and grant him peace, said that it has the weight of a third of the whole Qur'an. After the Fatihah (without whose recitation none of the Five Prayers are valid), it is the most frequently recited part of the Qur'an. Practising Muslims are likely to have recited it thousands or tens of thousands of times by the end of their lives.

Ikhlas means sincerity but also purity, because sincerity and purity are inextricably linked with acceptance of Allah's indivisible oneness and pre-eternity. Refusal to accept this about Allah indicates insincerity and pollution.

The word 'Ahad' which Allah uses to describe Himself and is rendered above as Absolute Oneness is not just oneness in the sense of 'the number one' or 'one among many'. It is, linguistically and in the reality it indicates, absolute singularity, totally free of multiplicity and division. This cannot be encompassed by minds, however refined, because the mind is of the realm of multiplicity.

The doorway to witnessing Allah's Ahadiyya is submission, which is the meaning of the word Islam.

Allah says about Himself: "He has not given birth and was not born."

A Muslim would never use the word 'father'

to describe Allah. To do so would be considered a grave error suggesting an absence of belief, because it would be an untruth about the very foundation of existence. This is forbidden by Allah. Mistakes at the foundation mean great mistakes in words and actions. To say 'father' and 'son' in relation to the Divine is untrue.

'Isa, peace be upon him, was a slave of Allah and a Prophet whom Muslims love, revere and talk about often, relating his qualities and miracles, many of which are mentioned in the Qur'an. Careful Muslim speakers will not say his name without saying "'alayhi salam" – upon him peace. They consider it one of the worst actions to defame or slander him, may Allah protect him, just as they consider it an atrocity to say anything against any of the Prophets or Messengers and most especially the Prophet Muhammad, may Allah bless him and grant him peace.

Because what good can there be in insulting the best of people, the pinnacles of humanity, the ones who were unable to lie, the ones who were prepared by Allah to guide others, the ones who received Divine Revelation? What good can there be in insulting those without whom people would never have known how to worship or even live? What kind of person could insult Adam, Nuh

Christianity

(Noah), Ibrahim (Abraham), Musa (Moses), 'Isa (Jesus) and all of the other many, many prophets, some of whom we know about and many more of whom we do not? How could anyone permit their names to be used as swear-words, as is now endemic in the dominant society?

What kind of a heart could turn against these men once that heart has been made aware of their station? What kind of person, once informed of their standing with Allah and their standing among people, would not at least refrain from ugly comments, even if they cannot find it in their hearts to believe in what they brought?

Of all these men, Jesus, peace be upon him, was among the greatest. And his high station consisted precisely in his total slavehood to his Lord. The mistake the Christians had already made by the time Islam arrived, and for which they are censured in Qur'an, was to go too far in attributing greatness to their Prophet by elevating him to Divinity. If they had not done that, there would have been no need to call them to Islam or to include Jews in the universal command to Islam. The Jews would have continued to fall under the previously purifying command of Christianity. The people we call Jews today are those who, if indeed they follow anything, still reject the Prophet Jesus and reject Muhammad after him, peace be upon both of them. The Jews have insisted on staying with teachings that were already corrupted by the time 'Isa arrived, peace be upon him. The people we call Christians today are those who, if indeed they follow anything, have not heard or still refuse to accept the purifying message of Islam, which calls them back to worship of Allah, the Sublime Creator of the universe and Sender of Prophets and Messengers, Who has no partners or offspring and is far removed from the condition of mankind and every created thing, and to Whom their own Prophet called his followers, as had Moses, Ibrahim and every Prophet and Messenger before them.

Other races have had their own Prophets and Messengers, as can be seen in the fragments of teachings left over among the people of the Far East, the Native Americans and others, all of which, despite their sublimity, are just that: fragments, not whole ways of life that are still in a living condition upon which one can base one's own life, let alone a society.

Having said all this, the Christians and Jews are still some of the closest people to us as Muslims and we have special respect for them inasmuch as they live on the basis of what they still have. But it would be wrong to say that Islam is one of the 'three monotheistic religions'. To put Islam on any kind of equivalent footing with those religions as they are now constituted is like comparing the living with the dead. They may have once been of the same category, and some features may be the same, but the former can be relied on while the others cannot.

Some Muslims have been promoting the misguided concept of 'interfaith dialogue' and of a brotherhood of mankind and a universality of religions, and of everyone believing in the same god – or that Judaism, Christianity and Islam are three faiths of some kind of equal standing. Even if this is done with the intention of diplomacy, or wanting to be friendly, or not wanting to be cast out or branded fundamentalist or Islamist or whatever the latest verbal weapon is to attack Islam and other religions – it is wrong. It denies sincere people the opportunity to know Allah and to know the sublime event of Prophethood and Messengership.

Islam is not a monotheistic religion. It is not a theism. It is not an -ism at all. It is not a concept among concepts. That kind of reductionist categorisation comes from Orientalists and other enemies of Islam and has been adopted by some

Muslims, especially ones educated in the teaching arenas run and financed by those people.

Islam is not a concept. Revelation is:

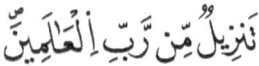

Sent down from the Lord of the Worlds.

To rank it among other religions means the one doing the ranking has not seen it for what it is: a call from Reality and an invitation to see. This means, if you are a seeker and a seer, it is a call to you.

If you are a Christian, the message Islam has for you is that it encompasses all of the things in Christianity that are right and allows the mistakes that man later introduced into the teachings of the Prophet 'Isa, peace be upon him, to be set aside. Salvation is not simply by believing in 'Isa, peace be upon him. We will be judged according to our actions and the intentions behind them.

If you intend to do one good action and then do it, you will be rewarded twice: once for the intention and once for the action itself. If you intend to do a good action but don't end up doing it, you will be rewarded once for your intention. If you intend to do a wrong action and do it, this will weigh against you once. If you intend to do a wrong action then refrain from it, you will be rewarded. Allah's Mercy is greater than our wrong actions.

'Isa, peace be upon him, was not crucified. We are told by the Messenger, may Allah bless him and grant him peace, that another man took his place and was made to appear like him. The Ascension, however, is true, in that Allah took 'Isa, peace be upon him, to Himself, in bodily form. The Prophet 'Isa will re-appear towards the end of time and will marry, have children and affirm the Messengership of Muhammad, his brother in Prophethood and pure natural belief. These are some of the things we are told by Muhammad, may Allah bless him and grant him peace.

QUR'AN

Qur'an means recitation. It is the Word of Allah.

Its words were sent down – which means they came into the world – in the purest Arabic language, by the intermediary of the Angel Jibril (Gabriel) into the heart of the Messenger Muhammad.

Such was the impact of the event of Revelation, of the descent of the Qur'an into the heart of the Messenger, that he perspired, went red, became agitated when it was happening.

The impact of Qur'an on those who heard it was profound.

'Umar ibn al-Khattab was one of the leading enemies of the Messenger of Allah and a man feared among his people. When he found out his sister and her husband had become Muslim, he went to their house to confront them, heard her reciting Qur'an and struck her so hard, she bled from the mouth. He then felt contrite and asked her to show him what she had been reciting. She replied that he was not Muslim and was therefore not allowed to touch the parchment on which it was written. He went out and washed himself, then she gave him it and he read a verse from the chapter of Ta Ha (20:14):

I am Allah.
There is no god but Me.
So worship Me.
And establish prayer
to remember Me.

This, confronting him at that particular place and time, in its peerless, inimitable Arabic, had such a powerful effect on him that he broke down in tears.

He went straight to the house where the Messenger of Allah had been staying and became Muslim.

The Qur'an was revealed, often but not always in response to particular circumstances and events, over a period of twenty-three years.

A complete written copy of the revealed Word of Allah was first compiled into one physical book in the time of the third Khalif, 'Uthman ibn Affan, fifteen years after the death of the Messenger of Allah, may Allah bless him and grant him peace; its collation had already been decided on by the preceding two Khalifs, Abu Bakr and 'Umar, who had appointed the aforementioned Companion Zayd ibn Thabit, at that time still young, to do it. He had been the scribe of the Messenger of Allah, may Allah bless him and grant him peace.

Ever since its Revelation, those who heard it and believed in it realised its supreme importance and committed it to memory, either wholly or in part, and the practice of memorisation became established everywhere the Muslims spread. There are still now countries in which the majority of men and a large proportion of women have memorised the whole Book by the time they reach maturity. The Mus-haf, the written copy of the Revelation, is an aid and a helper but not the primary means by which the Qur'an is known. The primary means are the memories and hearts of the Believers. The chains of transmission by which people learn Qur'an are themselves memorised much like the chains of Tasawwuf, reaching right back to the Messenger of Allah, may Allah bless him and grant him peace, so that people know the names of all the people through whom it has reached them from him, may Allah bless him and grant him peace.

All around the world there are millions, perhaps billions of printed and written copies of the Book of Allah, in mosques, libraries and people's homes, all in the original language. Translations also exist to aid people in accessing its meanings if they are not fluent in Arabic.

There is no dispute in the Muslim world about what is in the Qur'an. It is universally known and accepted in its original language.

The careful Muslim who needs to dispose of a copy of the Qur'an for whatever reason, or to dispose of paper on which any of it is written, or indeed on which the Name of Allah is written, does not throw it in the rubbish. He burns it. That is the acceptable means of disposal, taking the transcribed words out of the realm of impurity, since fire purifies. So when the enemies of Islam burn copies of the Qur'an with the intention of insulting and offending Muslims and stating that they do not accept them or it, the Muslim educated in his Deen, while rightly sensing the intended insult, at least can feel relief that it is out of the enemies' hands and consigned to a proper end. They cannot burn the Qur'an, which is the Word of Allah. They can only burn the physical transcripts of it. My Master related:

> When word came to a remote Muslim village in China that Mao's Revolutionary Guards were coming to burn their Mushafs, the Imam assembled all the children and began to teach them to recite the Qur'an. When the Guards finally arrived they were met by smiling villagers in front of a pile of Copies. As the Guards set fire to the books the sounds of a hundred children came from the mosque reciting the blessed words of the Qur'an.

MARRIAGE

The Messenger of Allah, may Allah bless him and grant him peace, married and encouraged marriage. He said, "Marriage is half the Deen."

This has an outward reason and an inward reason.

Outwardly, marriage in Islam is an agreement between a man and a woman that they may live together and have sexual relations. In it the woman is afforded financial, social and physical protection. The children which in most cases ensue from a marriage are also protected financially and socially, as is their inheritance. Both parties in the marriage are afforded protection in their intimate needs, since sexual relations may not be withheld by either person.

Marriage, in which the Prophet Muhammad was the foremost example, is the coming-together of two opposite human forms – male and female – in a Prophetically, therefore Divinely, legitimised way.

The Muslim couple, in its highest expression, is a collaborative union within agreed-upon parameters. They know what marriage is for and what it is not for. Contrary to what is put about against Islam by those in whose interests it is that the female half of humanity should be 'free' to enhance the productivity of the dominant economic system, there are no laws telling Muslim women they have to stay at home. Her property and any income she has, however great, do not belong to men. Most couples produce children, which is a large part of what marriage is for. As a result, many women have their centre of gravity around the household, because, still in touch with their nature, they incline to be there for their children and support their husbands who, for their part, protect and provide for them. It is a synergy. With a definite legal and economic framework.

Islam has been attacked because it is supposed to deny women their rights. This, from a society that has turned women into pseudo-men and men into pseudo-women, or even post-gender units, as if one's sex is something to be evolved out of. Massive amounts of money are spent propagating a vision of man and woman as identical. This has harmed women and men.

The Muslim man may marry up to four wives. This means the Muslim woman has the theoretical biological choice of any Muslim man as mate, protector and companion, except those few men who are already taken by four women. And it means there is no excuse for irresponsible male sexual adventure.

Both men and women benefit from knowing that their spouses will in all but the most unusual cases not engage in sex outside marriage, not primarily because of the punishments for transgression, which are fierce, but because they fear Allah and wish to live as Muslims live and, even if they lose sight of that, because of the containing forces of social approval and disapproval. And, in a fully functioning Muslim society, as has existed at different times in the past, because of the last resort of the law.

Divorce, although strongly disliked, is available for marriages that prove dysfunctional or untenable.

Because of this overall framework of marriage, children know who their parents are and are likely to receive their rightful inheritance, which is another thing precisely set out by the limits of Allah and His Messenger, all of which are pure wisdom and have been recorded with great clarity. So while inheritance will always contain the possibility of dispute, the basic pattern is set out legally and one's estate may not be used posthumously as a weapon of punishment or reward. Disinheritance is not permitted. Everyone's due is clearly laid down by the Shari'a of Islam.

That is the legal framework. But the main substance of relations between spouses in Islam is courtesy and sweetness. Allah the Exalted says in the Qur'an, Surat al-Baqara 186, about the relationship between men and women:

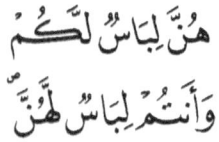

> They are clothing for you
> and you for them.

Ibn Kathir said, "It was the character of the Prophet to conduct himself in a beautiful manner with his wives, being cheerful and kind to them, generously spending on them, and laughing with them."

He, may Allah bless him and grant him peace, said of his first wife, the affluent noblewoman Khadijah, may Allah be pleased with her, who employed him as her agent in trade before they were married: "She believed in me when the whole world refuted me and she attested to my veracity when the whole world accused me of falsehood. She offered me compassion and loyalty with her wealth when everyone else had forsaken me."

Aisha, may Allah be pleased with her, was asked: "What did the Messenger of Allah, may Allah bless him and grant him peace, do in his house?" She said: "He was a human being like any other; he would clean his garments, milk his sheep and serve himself."

She said, may Allah be pleased with her, "The Prophet, may Allah bless him and grant him peace, would call for a drink and insist that I take it first before he drank from it. So I would take it and drink from it, then put it down, then he would take it and drink from it, putting his mouth where mine had been on the cup."

Aisha, may Allah be pleased with her, reported that she was with the Prophet, peace and blessings be upon him, on a journey. She said, "I raced him on foot and I outran him, but when I gained some weight, I raced him again and he outran me. The Prophet said: 'This is for that other race.'"

The Messenger of Allah told men to play with their wives and be sweet with them: "You play with her and she plays with you, and you laugh with her and she laughs with you, and you joke with her and she jokes with you."

He said, may Allah bless him and grant him peace, "None of you should come on to his wife like an animal; but rather there should be between them a messenger." It was said, "What is the messenger, O Prophet of Allah?" He replied, "Kisses and sweet words."

Essentially, while marriage is on the outside contractual, its everydayness is having good manners with each other, serving and helping each other in the variegated ways men and women serve and help each other, being loyal to one another and protecting one another and one another's property and name, relaxing with each other and enjoying leisure with each other, enjoying intimacy with one another, being light with each other and reflecting with each other.

And collaborating in actions that serve the wider community.

WAR

War is a function of the human creature. The question is not whether there should be war, but under what conditions, and what are its limits?

Humanist wars have perhaps been some of the cruellest, most indiscriminately destructive and most hypocritical in history. The wars waged by the United States are a good example, especially because advocates of the United States, both within it and elsewhere, put it forward as the upholder of virtue and claim the country as a bastion of Human Rights, Democracy and other humanist doctrines.

The existence of the United States is based

on the genocide of its indigenous peoples. The United States is, at the time of writing, the only nation ever to have obliterated whole cities full of humans using nuclear bombs. Their waging of war, directly and by proxy, has continued before and since, bringing their ideological idols of Freedom, Democracy and Human Rights.

In the years between 2001 and 2021 the United States and its allies dropped or fired a total of 337,055 bombs and missiles on other countries. There were around eleven million deaths in wars waged under the leadership of Tony Blair, George Bush and Barack Obama. It is beyond the scope of this book to go into details of American humanist warfare. The point is that it is the media apparatus of this ultra-violent national entity called the USA, its personnel and its allies, that has intentionally built up a picture of Islam as a violent religion.

Put their media-conjured picture aside and approach Islam for yourself, through your own experience. If you have no such experience, seek it out with honesty and you will find out for yourself. Go to the Muslims, if you have the courage of your convictions, and find out.

Islam has guidance for trade, washing, burying the dead, eating, travelling, praying, greeting, and every other primary human activity, including war. This is what makes it unique. Especially now. Other religions have lost this, so they have had to resort at best to a rhetoric of peace while having nothing useful to say about war. In doing so they become tacit allies in wars without limits, because they sequester in a pacifist prison that true impulse in the human creature which would naturally set limits on and give guidance to war.

The rules of warfare in Islam are strict. Muslims have no permission from Allah to fight when greatly outnumbered and when there is no realistic prospect of victory. They are not permitted to kill women, children or old people in war, unless those people are actively engaged in fighting them. They may not rape or mutilate.

There are clear laws governing what is done with booty, what is done with captured people and how captured lands are divided up. All of these are from the Prophetic source.

Muslims may not wage individualistic campaigns without leadership and without the Banner of Islam held high. They are not permitted to commit suicide, including as a means of attacking others. The tactic of suicide bombing is forbidden in Islam. The judgment that the Messenger tells us awaits the suicide is that they will find themselves performing the self-murdering act on themselves for ever. Suicide has no place in Islam.

The opposite of suicide is fighting with nobility in the face of great danger in the expectation of a great outcome, while not knowing whether you will survive. That is something which almost every society has always condoned, recognised and admired as one of the highest activities available to the human being, decorated with the highest honours.

The spread of Islam in its beginnings, whereby it reached Iberia and China in less than a hundred years, involved a combination of military campaigns, emigration, diplomacy and trade by people whose society had become, in the shortest of time, clearly superior to everything around it. The military campaigns were mostly pitched battles between armies whose members volunteered to fight (conscription is forbidden in Islam) and in which the casualties were, by today's standards, miniscule. The Muslims were overwhelmingly victorious in the majority of these battles, which often led to treaties followed by either the installation of Muslim leadership over the newly subdued place, or the affirmation of existing leadership under the overall rule of the Muslims. The people of these places subsequently became Muslim through all the natural means by which they still become Muslim today, a process sometimes rapid and sometimes gradual. Primarily this means recognising Islam as a superior way of life and seeing that it refines and ennobles its adherents, both materially and spiritually. And discovering that it answers the inherent need for a transactional framework that accords with belief in God.

The idea that whole nations were forcibly 'converted' then somehow at some later point became settled in their Deen is an invention of the enemies of Islam.

War can never be made pleasant or romantic, but neither can its place be denied among the many activities in which humans engage. The balanced person would prefer to wage it on a sound basis, shown to us by the best of human beings, rather than for the reasons and in the ways it is conducted almost everywhere today, by people and leaders who send others to fight while themselves staying out of danger, then claim to bring peace and freedom while destroying whole countries, societies and peoples, lying, and appropriating the resources of the whole world.

THE JUDGMENT

Whether you die in war or in peace, you will be judged by Allah and you will be judged fairly. Not an atom's weight of wrong will ultimately be done to you in the final adding-up.

What does this mean, that we will be judged? It means that you are, at any given moment, the sum total of what you have done, and when your life is over, that will be what goes with you to where you go. Allah tells us in the Qur'an that at the end of time, we will be given our book in which our actions are written.

If this is hard for the modern mind to accept, consider its opposite. Is it feasible that your actions do not accrue with you? Even by the measure of the Science which we are told we must obey, it is impossible that they do not, since every action has a consequence and changes the things in contact with it. The physicality of an action has a consequence, both in the outside world and in the one who does it. The intention behind it also has a consequence in the unseen of the outside world and the unseen of the one who does it. To deny this is to deny the existence of intention and the existence of the unseen, the unseen simply meaning that there is an aspect of man and the rest of existence that the eyes do not perceive. It is a denial of the conscience, for what is conscience but a faculty Allah has given us to warn us against our own wrongs? The one who ignores or blocks out his conscience is headed for a particular kind of outcome: we all know this at some level. So do not deny the ultimate expression of this: your essence, stripped of the dimensions of time and space, will be confronted with the sum total of what you did and intended.

And Allah's forgiveness and Mercy encompass our own actions, good and bad.

Allah tells us about the Fire and the Garden.

The Judgment

Those who persist in doing wrong will be in the former once time is over, and those who do right will be in the latter. The decision is with Allah alone. Neither Muslims nor anybody else will stand in judgment over anyone else, nor over themselves. But when the time comes, we will be given to know the truth about our own actions. Those who did good will be grateful to Allah that they did it and those who did not will rue that they did not.

To deny the possibility of the Fire and the Garden is to deny the very existence of goodness and badness. It is nihilism: it is believing in nothing. Rightness and wrongness have no meaning if understood in material terms alone, because if they only exist as a construct of man's making, then anyone could decide for themselves what is right and wrong and it would not matter and could be proven not to matter. All of us, provided we are not mentally sick, know deep down that things do matter.

For the one who hears about Allah and about His Messenger, and responds – the Garden awaits them, consisting of every thing truly agreeable to the human creature, stripped of the containing attribute of time. There will be no suffering in it whatsoever. It is bliss. It has no beginning or end. It exists outside time for those who deserve it, which is up to Allah alone and is not for any priesthood to judge.

There are people in this world who remind you of the Garden and there are people in this world who remind you of the Fire.

When you are with the people of the Garden, you feel a happiness which is not about them as such, although it is by them that it comes upon you. This is the scent of the Garden.

From the people of the Fire, when you are with them, you sense a darkness that is very much about them and whatever you have invested in them. The Muslim is taught by the Messenger to avoid such people and have nothing to do with them.

The Messenger of Allah said that if you spend time with people, you become one of them. Once you are Muslim, the surest way of entering the Garden – and Allah knows best – is to be with its people. In their company it is easy to do good actions.

Be with the people who carry the scent of the Garden.

But if you spend time with them while refusing to become Muslim, you are someone who will not take what Allah is offering you.

To enter the company of the practising Muslims is to enter into a circle of people who are striving to abandon orientation towards anything in the world, even if they are fully in the world. It is a relief after burden. It is adventure. When the sublime responsibility of Islam is realised, it is exciting. It is to discover brotherhood and sisterhood higher and closer than the bonds of blood or battle. It is to understand what it is to be truly human, because the Muslims are a people who agree on and understand the reason why we are here. They can enjoy life to the full, indeed more fully than without this knowledge. As they get older, they don't go downhill, deteriorating until death. They get better. They mature. They gain wisdom. They grow in light. They increase in serenity. Accompanying them is a joy which, once tasted and savoured, you will never want to be without. They have a portion of Prophethood, inherited from the Best of Creation, Muhammad, may Allah bless him and grant him peace.

ISLAM IS WITH THE MUSLIMS, NOT IN BOOKS

This book is intended as a signpost. But Islam does not reside in books.

Every human takes a guide. Even if you are alone in a hut in the forests of beyond who has not seen a soul for years, you still have yourself as company. You take yourself as a guide.

To say you need nobody's help along the way, nobody to show you how to live, is basically saying you prefer your own opinion to that of everyone else. If you think you know better than everyone else, then Islam is not for you.

If, however, you sense that this is not the case, despite or perhaps precisely while recognising ability in yourself, then seek out the people of the Garden. They are the Muslims.

The rightly-guided Muslim is not in reaction to the dominant society. He is neither terrorist, nor pacifist. Neither apologist, nor antagonist. Neither running away from this world, nor running towards it. Not afraid, nor reckless. Neither obsessed with wealth, nor obsessed with poverty. He has not made Islam his culture or his idol. He has made Islam the filter for his culture and the destroyer of his idols. He is drawing from the Timeless Source.

Such people: seek out their company. If you set out for them, you will find them. If you seek knowledge of Allah and are prepared to lay down what you know and free your hands to receive something new, you will get knowledge.

May the peace of Allah be upon you, and His mercy and blessings.

www.ingramcontent.com/pod-product-compliance
Lightning Source LLC
Chambersburg PA
CBHW022014290426
44109CB00015B/1171